PRAISE FOR

THIS BOOK IS OVERDUE!

"With this joyful and absorbing look into the world of librarians, Johnson has filled a desperately needed gap in our understanding, and she will inspire her readers to feel as she does: thank goodness for librarians."

—*Chicago Sun-Times*

"[A] humorous, unabashed love letter to the men and women who used to toil quietly in stacks but now circulate in cyberspace."

—*USA Today*

"Gloriously geeky ... Energetic, winningly acerbic and downright fun, *This Book Is Overdue* will leave you convinced that librarians really can save the world."

—BookPage.com

"Johnson's exquisite book taps into the radical changes that libraries are going through. She blows apart the librarian stereotypes."

—*Newark Star-Ledger*

"She pays homage to a profession undergoing a mind-boggling transition. . . . This cheerful book is full of personalities."

—*Plain Dealer*

"Johnson has made her way to the secret underbelly of librarianship, and the result is both amazing and delightful. Savvy, brave, hip, brilliant, these are not your childhood librarians. And who better to tell their stories than the sly, wise Marilyn Johnson."   —Mary Roach, author of *Stiff*

"As Johnson amply shows in her romp through the brave new world of the profession, [the] new librarians *cum* information scientists are building on the work of their pioneering predecessors as they branch out in sometimes surprising directions."   —*Boston Globe*

"To those who have imagined a dalliance with a librarian— and there are millions of us—Marilyn Johnson's new book, chocked as it is full of strange, compelling stories, offers insight into the wildness behind the orderly façade of the humans who are at the controls of our information."
          —Pete Dexter, author of *Paris Trout* and *Spooner*

"Ms. Johnson's enthusiasm for libraries and the people who work in them is refreshingly evident."
          —*Wall Street Journal*

"Because of Johnson's bright personality and the brightness she finds in her subject, her book is charming, fairly brimming with ain't-it-cool news. But her underlying message is serious and cautionary."   —*Philadelphia Inquirer*

"Johnson's characters desperately care about half-forgotten brawlers, freedom fighters, and canine celebrities. They are the guardians of all there is to know. It doesn't matter whether they carry on their efforts in analog or digital format. For they are waging the holy battle to resurrect the entire world, over and over again, in its entirety—keeping every last tidbit safe and acid free."

—Pagan Kennedy, *New York Times Book Review*

"Johnson does for the library profession what Malcolm Gladwell did for the theory of memetics in *The Tipping Point.*"

—Nora Rawlinson, *EarlyWord*

"Is this book overdue? Yes, but perhaps it's still in the nick of time."

—*Minneapolis Star Tribune*

About the Author

Rob Fleder

MARILYN JOHNSON owns multiple library cards and uses them often. As a staff writer for *Life*, she specialized in writing obituaries of celebrities who weren't quite dead. Her first book, *The Dead Beat: Lost Souls, Lucky Stiffs, and the Perverse Pleasures of Obituaries*, was a Borders Original Voices selection and a finalist for the Barnes & Noble Discover Great New Writers Award. She lives with her husband, Rob Fleder, and their family in the Hudson Valley in New York.

JOHNSON, MARILYN

THIS BOOK IS OVERDUE!

How Librarians and Cybrarians Can Save Us All

HARPER  PERENNIAL

NEW YORK • LONDON • TORONTO • SYDNEY • NEW DELHI • AUCKLAND

HARPER ● PERENNIAL

A hardcover edition of this book was published in 2010 by Harper, an imprint of HarperCollins Publishers.

FIRST HARPER PERENNIAL EDITION PUBLISHED 2011.

Designed by Eric Butler

The Library of Congress has published the hardcover edition as follows:

Johnson, Marilyn, 1954–
    This book is overdue! : how librarians and cybrarians can save us all / Marilyn Johnson.—1st ed.
       p.   cm.
    Includes bibliographical references.
    ISBN 978-0-06-143160-9
    1. Libraries and society. 2. Libraries and the Internet. 3. Librarians— Effect of technological innovations on. 4. Libraries—Anecdotes.
5. Librarians—Anecdotes. 6. Library science—Anecdotes. I. Title.
Z716.4J64   2010
021.2—dc22

                                                          2010007860

ISBN 978-0-06-143161-6 (pbk.)

11 12 13 14 15 OV/RRD   10 9 8 7 6 5 4 3 2 1

To Dave and Dotty Johnson

Show me a computer expert who gives a damn,
and I'll show you a librarian.

—*Patricia Wilson Berger, former president, ALA*

CONTENTS

A blast of a six-shooter in the Wild West town of Deadwood sends us galloping into the world of librarians who wrangle paper history and digital information, and cartoon librarians who move and speak in real time on your computer screen . . . how obituaries of librarians are tracking the changes in this topsy-turvy profession . . . a silly and scurrilous entry on Wikipedia stands in for the mutating web . . . and we cast an eye over some of the stories of heroic librarians and archivists this book will tell

Frothing at the mouth and keeling over from too much information: science fiction or modern affliction? . . . on trying to understand social networking and turning to reference librarians for enlightenment . . . who needs librarians in the age of Google? we do! . . . the fools who projected the death of libraries . . . computers level the information playing field, and librarians are their keepers

The uneasy alliance between librarians and the computer experts they rely on as it plays out during a calamitous computer upgrade of the online catalog in Westchester County, NY—complete with an apocalyptic storm! . . . librarians, pressured to get out front with technology, scramble to retrain themselves . . . and a few outlaw librarians drive the tech guys crazy

You might not think of them as mouthy and opinionated, but librarians have taken to the blogosphere with a vengeance, networking, entertaining, instructing, and venting . . . yes, they are venting, viciously and hilariously, about you, their patrons . . . don't judge them until you, too, have cleaned up the poop in the book drop

An encounter at a glitzy benefit with two heroes of the library world turns into a visit with the Connecticut Four, in which three librarians and a tech guy recount their 1984-style nightmare as "John Doe," who sued the government to keep their patrons' records private

Librarians at St. John's University in Queens, New York, give students from developing nations, some of whom have never used a computer, enough tech training to pursue a long-distance master's degree and join the global conversation on human rights . . . a visit to Rome, where the librarians crash-train one group and graduate another

Librarians to the barricades! Anarchist librarians leave the building and hit the street, using smart phones and library databases to fight rumors and panic with trustworthy information for protestors . . . a visit with the librarian who helped launch Radical Reference and works to expand library service for those who live off the grid and to preserve their self-published stories

8.   Follow That Tattooed Librarian 123

Our enduring and, frankly, absurd fascination with sexy librarians and that
shushing business, and how some librarians deal with it . . . welcome to
the exotic world of librarians who mock themselves by performing precision
drills with book carts . . . and to pink-haired, tattooed librarians downing
cocktails while ear-splitting music shatters that stereotype

9.   Wizards of Odd 133

In which your author becomes an embedded reporter among librarians
in the virtual reality site of Second Life, and discovers the vibrant and
gender-bending world of international librarians who meet in the 3-D
Web's corridors and dark alleys to share resources and provide reference
service to other avatars

10.   Gotham City 171

A close look at the librarians of the venerable New York Public Library as
they hurtle at warp speed into the digital age . . . the reference librarian
who helps techno-stressed writers . . . the keeper of the treasures in a
crumbling kingdom of scholarship . . . the digital guru . . . the guardian of
black history . . . the arts and crafts librarian . . . and we discover which
of them survives the great transition

11.   What's Worth Saving? 213

Toni Morrison's house burns, and is anyone worried about her son? No, it's
her manuscripts everybody cares about . . . a course in literary archives
using the papers of a writer considerably more obscure than Morrison . . .
advice from an archivist on a personal mission . . . how the world's most

extensive collection of boxing artifacts survived hurricanes, fire, mold, and rats, thanks to a librarian who loves boxing and a boxing archivist . . . the difference between librarians and archivists, and how archivists are dealing with the digital age . . . creative innovations from the Library of Congress . . . yet another way information professionals save us

Outside in the cold with a crowd of happy revelers on a Saturday morning, waiting for the thrill of the opening of a new library . . . the recession-battered town of Darien, Connecticut, celebrates not just the new building, its dazzling design and user-friendly technology, but its librarians, who promote "extreme customer service" and who throw open the door to taxpaying locals and free-loading strangers alike

THIS BOOK IS OVERDUE!

1.

THE FRONTIER

In tough times, a librarian is a terrible thing to waste.

Down the street from the library in Deadwood, South Dakota, the peace is shattered several times a day by the noise of gunfire—just noise. The guns shoot blanks, part of an historic re-creation to entertain the tourists. Deadwood is a far tamer town than it used to be, and it has been for a good long while. Its library, that emblem of civilization, is already more than a hundred years old, a Carnegie brick structure, small and dignified, with pillars outside and neat wainscoting in. The library director is Jeanette Moodie, a brisk mom in her early forties who earned her professional degree online. She's gathering stray wineglasses from the previous night's reception for readers and authors, in town for the South Dakota Festival of Books. Moodie points out the portraits of her predecessors that hang in the front room. The first director started this library for her literary ladies' club in 1895, not long after the period that gives the modern town its flavor; she looks like a proper lady, hair piled on her head, tight bodice, a choker around her neck. Moodie is a relative blur. She runs the library and its website, purchases and catalogs the items in its collections, keeps the doors open more than forty hours a week, and hosts programs like the party, all with only part-time help. When she retires, she'll put on one of her neat suits, gold earrings, and rectangular glasses and sit still long enough to be captured for a portrait of her own.

Moodie is also the guardian of a goldmine, the history of a town that relies on history for its identity. She oversees an archive of rare books and genealogical records, which, when they're not being read under her supervision, are kept locked up in the South Dakota Room of the library. Stored in a vault off the children's reading room downstairs are complete sets of local newspapers dating back to 1876 that document Deadwood's colorful past in real time. A warning on the library website puts their contents in a modern context: "remember that political correctness did not exist in 19th-century Deadwood—many terms used ['negro minstrelcy,' for instance, and 'good injun'] are now considered derogatory or slanderous, but are a true reflection of our history."

If you want a gauge of how important this archive is to Deadwood, Moodie will take you into the vault, a virtually impregnable room lined with concrete and secured by a heavy steel door. No fire or earthquake or thief is going to get at the good stuff inside this place. A dehumidifier hums by the door. Newsprint and sepia photos, stored in acid-free, carefully labeled archival boxes, are stacked neatly on shelves around a big worktable. In her spare time, the librarian comes down here to browse the old articles that a consultant has been indexing, systematically listing the subjects and titles of each story for the library's electronic catalog. The town's past lives on in this catalog, linked with all the other libraries in South Dakota. Anyone can log on as a guest, consult the library's index online, and learn that the *Black Hills Daily Times* published a story in 1882 called "Why Do We Not Have Library & Reading Rooms?" and three years later, "Reading Room and Library Almost Complete," alongside stories like "Accidental Shooting Part of a Free for All" and "Cowboys Shoot Up Resort."

Moodie, like her predecessor a century ago, is essentially organizing the past and making it available to the citizenry, but she's doing so in ways that the librarian of the late 1800s could never have imagined, preserving images of one frontier with the tools of another. What would the proper lady in the portrait make of the current librarian's tasks, the maintenance of the website, for instance, with its ghostly and omniscient reach?

There's another Deadwood library on the digital frontier. This one doesn't resemble the elegant Carnegie building in the real town in South Dakota—it looks instead like a crude wooden storefront—but it, too, evokes the period that characterizes Deadwood, the late 1800s, the gold rush, and the Wild West. The difference is that this library exists solely on the Internet in the virtual world known as Second Life. People at computers around the globe, taking the form of avatars dressed in chaps and boots or long prairie dresses and playing the roles of prospectors, saloon keepers, and ordinary citizens, can visit the library in an historic reenactment of Deadwood in Second Life. They can enter this ramshackle building and, by typing questions in a chat box, ask the librarian what sort of outfit a prostitute would have worn, or where to find information on panning for gold. Or they can browse the collection the librarian has gathered in the form of links to dime novels and other old-time books, available in digital form from sites like Project Gutenberg and the Internet Archive.

The librarian, Lena Kjellar, shows up onscreen as a cartoon woman in a bustle skirt. The person behind this avatar was trained to provide Second Life reference services by a real-life reference librarian and is part of an information network anchored by hundreds of professional librarians who flock to this interactive site for fun and stay to volunteer their skills— they figure everyone should be able to use library services, even avatars. In fact, "Lena Kjellar" is a retired electrical engineer and locomotive buff from Illinois named Dave Mewhinney; he feels that taking on a woman's shape in Second Life makes him more approachable.

Somewhere between Jeanette Moodie's frontiers and Lena Kjellar's is the story of a profession in the midst of an occasionally mind-blowing transition. A library is a place to go for a reality check, a bracing dose of literature, or a "true reflection of our history," whether it's a brick-and-mortar building constructed a century ago or a fanciful arrangement of computer codes. The librarian is the organizer, the animating spirit behind it, and the navigator. Her job is to create order out of the confusion of the past, even as she enables us to blast into the future.

I became interested in librarians while researching my first book, about obituaries. With the exception of a few showy eccentrics, like the former soldier in Hitler's army who had a sex change and took up professional whistling, the most engaging obit subjects were librarians. An obituary of a librarian could be about anything under the sun, a woman with a phenomenal memory, who recalled the books her aging patrons read as children—and was also, incidentally, the best sailor on her stretch of the Maine coast—or a man obsessed with maps, who helped automate the Library of Congress's map catalog and paved the way for wonders like Google Maps.

There were visionaries like Frederick Kilgour, the first to combine libraries' catalogs in one computerized database back in the early seventies. This was a great act in the history of knowledge—its efficient and useful multiplication. Under Kilgour's direction, what began as a few dozen college libraries in Ohio sharing their catalogs soon snowballed into a world catalog, the Online Computer Library Center. Now anyone can go to WorldCat.org, the OCLC's catalog of a gazillion library records, and find many libraries that carry the item you need; WorldCat has made every computer a portal to institutions from the Library of Congress to the Tauranga (New Zealand) District Library. Kilgour lived to the age of ninety-two and taught till he was ninety. His obituarist noted that during World War II, "like many librarians . . . [he] gravitated into intelligence work." Good librarians are natural intelligence operatives. They possess all of the skills and characteristics required for that work: curiosity, wide-ranging knowledge, good memories, organizational and analytical aptitude, and discretion.

I met Judith Krug, another visionary librarian, in the course of my research. Krug fought censorship for four decades while running the Office for Intellectual Freedom in the Chicago headquarters of the American Library Association (ALA). She was tiny, beautifully turned out, and ferociously clear about the librarian's role in fighting censorship. I didn't realize until I read her untimely obituary that Krug had launched Banned Books Week back in the eighties, a bold and pointed celebration of everything from *Huckleberry Finn* to trash and political incitement. The banners flying in my public library the last week of September each year had been dreamed up by her.

But the first in a long list of memorialized librarians who made me want to inhabit this world was Henriette Avram. She beckoned from the obits page, with her mysterious, knowing smile, the chain-smoking systems analyst who automated the library records of the Library of Congress and wrote the first code for computerized catalogs (MARC—*Ma*chine *R*eadable *C*ataloging), a form of which is still used today. She inspired a generation of women to combine library work and computers. Her intellectual daughters and sons met after she died to pay her tribute, wearing giant buttons edged in black ribbon, bearing the image of their gray-haired heroine and the legend *Mother of MARC*.

Whether the subject was a community librarian or a prophet, almost every librarian obituary contained some version of this sentence: "Under her watch, the library changed from a collection of books into an automated research center." I began to get the idea that libraries were where it was happening—wide open territory for innovators, activists, and pioneers.

The profession that had once been the quiet gatekeeper to discreet palaces of knowledge is now wrestling a raucous, multiheaded, madly multiplying beast of exploding information and information delivery systems. Who can we trust? In a world where information itself is a free-for-all, with traditional news sources going bankrupt and publishers in trouble, we need librarians more than ever. We might not need a librarian to tell us that the first chapter of the Wikipedia entry about a Red Sox ballplayer, which we happened to look up during a slow moment of a Boston blowout of the Yankees, was scurrilous mischief: "[He] keeps his beard grown out to hide a rare birth defect. [He] was born with a huge vagina where a normal human chin would be. This would explain . . . why [he] is constantly fidgeting around in his beard because yeast infections are common in chin vaginas." This passage disappeared from Wikipedia in minutes, but not before I'd preserved a screen shot of the page and my printer had spit out a copy. Chin vaginas! What next? But in this age of mutating wikis, how much else is untrue? With the same number of keystrokes, I could have found more than a dozen articles in a database on my local library's website, and called up any of them using my library card. Or I could have summoned a librarian via one of the chat services that proliferate on the Web, like the one at the Boston Public Library that offers "24/7 reference—A Professional Librarian, on Your Computer, at Your Convenience." I didn't need a card to claim the undivided attention of a professional who made it her job to find me reliable information, whether it was about something as important as a Supreme Court decision or as frivolous as a baseball player's beard.

Librarians' values are as sound as Girl Scouts': truth, free speech, and universal literacy. And, like Scouts, they possess a quality that I think makes librarians invaluable and indispensable: they want to *help*. They want to help *us*. They want to be of service. And they're not trying to sell us anything. But as one librarian put it, "The wolf is always at the door." In tight economic times, with libraries sliding farther and farther down the list of priorities, we risk the loss of their ideals, intelligence, and knowledge, not to mention their commitment to access for all— librarians consider free access to information the foundation of democracy, and they're right. Librarians are essential players in the information revolution because they level that field. They enable those without money or education to read and learn the same things as the billionaire and the Ph.D. In prosperous libraries, they loan out laptops; in strapped ones, they dole out half hours of computer time. They are the little "d" democrats of the computer age who keep the rest of us wired.

In tough times, a librarian is a terrible thing to waste.

When the School of Library Science at Rutgers University became the School of Information Science in early 2009, a change the Universities of Michigan, Syracuse, California–Berkeley, and others had already made, it was announcing that computers had taken over part of the curriculum. "Information science" is code for "don't worry, we're not dinosaurs; we've got the electronic age covered." About a third of the library graduate programs in the United States have now ditched the word *library*. Not that librarians, as a rule, have begun identifying themselves as *information scientists*, or, for that matter, *cybrarians*—I use this last word to conjure up the new breed of tech-savvy librarians, part cyborg, part cat's-eye reading glasses. Unless librarians take jobs with exotic and semi-contrived names like *digital media specialist* or *metadata and information architect*, or, as the city of Edinburgh tried to (seriously) rename its librarians, *audience development specialists*, they are, mainly, and I hope forever, librarians.

Although this book starts and ends in public libraries on the East Coast, where I live, the story stretches across the country and beyond. We're all connected. What happens in one place is happening in another—or it will be. I walked into my local library one day to find it had come to a complete standstill while the cataloging software was upgraded. Remember libraries without computers? I could, but only barely. It was an eerie step back in time, and was, as it turned out, a fitting illustration of the intimate and sometimes strained relationship between professionals who serve the public and professionals who serve machines. No matter how tech savvy my local librarians have become, like the rest of us, they rely on computer technicians to cope with the frustrations and challenges of ever-evolving software and hardware. Incorporating the new technology while keeping the old material useful and accessible—this is just the latest task in the long list of librarians' tasks. That they manage this while holding firm to principles of free speech and the right to privacy is remarkable, which is why I wanted to visit the Connecticut librarians who challenged the FBI's right to examine the records of their patrons' computer searches. Theirs is a story not only about the triumph of the First and Fourth Amendments but also about what can be accomplished when librarians and computer experts work together as a team. They can stand up to the government.

This book can be read as a journey into increasingly activist and visionary forms of library work. The walls of the library have grown porous now and in some cases are merely virtual, as librarians have come out from behind their desks to serve as active enablers in the digital age. I found librarians who took to the streets alongside political protesters in order to provide them with immediate, vital, and reliable information, and academic librarians who have reached out to students halfway around the globe, teaching them the computer skills necessary to link them and their villages to the international human rights movement. But no matter where or how they use their training, members of this once quiet and private profession have taken to talking—and gossiping—on the Web. Early on, many of them recognized the potential of blogs as sources of information and training, and became bloggers themselves. Passionate, funny, and often profane, this crowd of computer-age librarians vent about their patrons while making wicked sport of themselves and those old jokes and stereotypes.

On every level, the field is bending and broadening, especially as it moves into cyberspace. Librarians are collaborating to create a universal network of virtual library services on the 3-D web. At the Library of Congress, with the largest holdings in the country, the staff continues to expand its collections with digital initiatives. Librarians there welcomed the first "born-digital" collection when they took charge of a trove of e-mails, voice mails, and other electronic artifacts gathered after the attacks of 9/11. Another behemoth, the New York Public Library system, is cooking up all sorts of digital projects, and at the same time addressing the needs of those who seem overwhelmed by technology. These include, perhaps surprisingly, artists and writers, whose works fill the shelves and archives of libraries everywhere.

At the often forgotten edges of library work, the archivists, those trying to capture history before it dissolves into the unrecorded past, toil in this transitional period that's turning out to be something of a dark age. It's not just mock wiki entries about chin vaginas that disappear almost as fast as they're created; hundreds of days of electronic messages from the Bush White House went missing for years, and only 14 million were recovered. *Only* 14 million! How do you manage such a massive and slippery outpouring? Fortunately, there are heroic archivists, librarians, cybrarians, and computer scientists determined to save the world, or at least a corner of it, whether it appears on an elusive flickering webpage or a sheet of dead wood.

This is a story about these professionals and their world, researched partly on a computer in mazes so extended and complex—every link a trapdoor to another set of links—that I never found a sturdy place to stop and grasp the whole. Information used to be scarce; now we're buried in it. We can copy the same piece of information in endless files, duplicating with abandon; we can have our info everywhere we want it, on little data sticks, on hard drives with remote backup software, in clouds in cyberspace. And yet, whole chapters of contemporary history are disappearing into the ether as e-mails get trashed and webpages are taken down and people die without sharing their passwords.

We know the first words uttered on the telephone, because Alexander Graham Bell wrote them down: "Mr. Watson. Come here. I need you." The first e-mail? As one of the digital histories points out, "In 1964, the first electronic mail message was sent from either the Massachusetts Institute of Technology, the Carnegie Institute of Technology or Cambridge University. The message does not survive, however, and so there is no documentary record to determine which group sent the pathbreaking message." Its contents are a mystery, a little smudge where history has been erased.

So where does one go in such a wobbly, elusive, dynamic, confusing age? Wherever the librarians and archivists are.

They're sorting it all out for us.

2.

INFORMATION SICKNESS

Late in the 1990s, I saw my local public libraries shake off their dust and stir to life. The new hardware was a crucial component, but no, really it was the librarians themselves who were making the difference.

I've lived in my house for ten years, and the books are crushing me. I've given away carloads, and still they reproduce. Somewhere in these disorderly shelves is a novel published in 1981 called *Easy Travel to Other Planets*. The novel, by Ted Mooney, was notorious when it came out because one character, a female marine biologist, has sex with a dolphin. For me, though, the most memorable passage is the description of the affliction from which the denizens of this slightly futuristic world suffer: *information sickness*. There is too much to take in. Their brains overload and they lose their senses.

If you don't know where to find a book, it might as well not exist. I couldn't find *Easy Travel* in my house. Ordinarily, if I wanted to consult a book I owned but couldn't put my hands on, I'd go on Amazon and use the neat *Search This Book* function: I would simply type in *information sickness,* and all the pages on which this phrase appears would be revealed. But this worked only for recently published books with cooperative publishers; *Easy Travel* was too old for that. So I went to the supercatalog at WorldCat.org, where, as promised by the obituary of Frederick Kilgour, the man who first combined the records of multiple libraries' catalogs, librarians were busily compiling one giant digital catalog of the world's books. You type in a title and get back a list of hundreds of libraries where that title can be found, beginning with the closest. I found 532 libraries that owned *Easy Travel,* listed in a concentric circle from where I happened to be, the "New York Public Library—Research," as WorldCat called the majestic library at Forty-second Street and Fifth Avenue. I could follow the digital breadcrumbs and track copies of the book through all five boroughs of New York City, moving on to the U.S. Military Academy Library at West Point (forty-four miles away, it informed me), followed by locations in the Midwest, the West, and the South. Then the list fanned out to Canada, Europe, and beyond, until finally, having exhausted all the closer possibilities, WorldCat found the book in the holdings of the University of Tasmania, more than ten thousand miles away.

Because I happened to be embedded in that big library in Manhattan, with access to a quiet room for writing this and maybe a million items tucked away on the other side of the wall, I checked its online catalog and verified that it owned a copy of *Easy Travel*. Oddly, the novel was on microfilm, and the librarians in the microfilm room had to light the lamps on their miners' hats to find it. Though it's a literary novel, *Easy Travel* had been stashed on a reel with a bunch of science fiction. Was there a shelf of sci-fi being dumped and this someone's defiant protest? No, it seemed I was holding a relic from the days when a former administrator, obsessed with space to store books, had the bright idea to throw batches of books together, patch up their contents on homemade reels of microfilm, then dump the physical books he'd had copied. He is not the hero of this book.

A typed list of a dozen or so novels appeared at the beginning of the microfilm reel and *Easy Travel* was among them. There were squiggles of dust on my viewing lens and the light in the room was dim; the pages had been microfilmed hastily, a few of them duplicated. I would give anything for one of those trademark library moments, sitting in a polished wood chair while sunlight slanted over my shoulder and I turned the pages of an old tome, blah blah blah. But here was my space-saving substitute, which required no fewer than four librarians and clerks to fetch and help thread into the machine. Squinting, I was able to make out the part where one of the characters in the book noted that "information sickness, like malaria, recurs unpredictably," and speculated that the president himself might be suffering this particular affliction ("he's certainly in the right risk bracket"). And then—oh joy!—there was the account of an information-sickness attack, a passage that has stayed in the back of my brain for all these years:

Jeffrey discovers a woman harmed by information excess. All the symptoms are present: bleeding from the nose and ears, vomiting, deliriously disconnected speech, apparent disorientation, and the desire to touch everything. She has a rubber mat rolled up under her arm and is walking around one of the soft new park benches recently installed by the city, palpating it hungrily. A small crowd has collected around her, listening to her complicated monologue: Birds of Prey Cards, sunspot souffle, Antarctic unemployment. Jeffrey hesitates. I've never seen one so far gone, he thinks. But, judging her young enough to warrant hope, he gently takes the rubber mat from the woman, unrolls it upon the pavement, and helps her to assume the memory-elimination posture. After a minute, the bleeding stops. "I was on my way to dance class," she says to him, still running her ravening fingers over his leather coat sleeves, "when suddenly I was dazzled. I couldn't tell where one thing left off and the next began."

Ha! "I couldn't tell where one thing left off and the next began." No kidding! Just as the novelist predicted, we were bleeding information from the nose and ears, though dazed and disoriented was not how I experienced it. Most of the time, I felt like I was three years old, high on chocolate cake and social networks, constantly wired, ingesting information and news about information, books and books about books, data and metadata—I was, in other words, overstimulated yet gluttonous for more. I spent days in the labyrinths of the Internet, watching webpages multiply onscreen at an even faster pace than the books and papers proliferated under my feet. From the outside I'm sure it looked like I needed help assuming the "memory-elimination posture," or possibly I needed an intervention, but I wouldn't want it any other way. Information and new forms of information were washing over me in oceans and it was fun to splash in the wake.

I had my limits. I often felt baffled and frustrated. I understood—I *thought* I understood—then things changed, or I learned the next thing that made everything I knew before obsolete. When I worked in an office, there was always a computer expert or two on staff to keep us connected and to untangle the USB wires and bewilderments. Having a tech department to consult, it turns out, is almost as valuable as having a doctor. Now, self-employed and unaffiliated with any computer scientists, without a sheltering institution to guide or rescue me, I'm challenged, like most people who aren't programmers. Where could we turn? Who could we consult who both understood and spoke our language?

Thank goodness for librarians.

I stood at the reference desk, my head buzzing. My old method of capturing the information on the Web wasn't working anymore. I had been copying text on websites and saving it to text files, but sometime around 2006, the Web took a leap into jazzed-up graphics and I began crashing my word-processing programs. What could I do? It wasn't enough to save the Web address; there was no guarantee I could get into the site later. How could I save content on the increasingly dynamic Web? The librarian I was consulting didn't blink. "Have you tried this?" she asked, showing me the pull down menu of her browser and choosing the option to "Save Page As." A box popped up, with the option "Save As Web Page." Click. It was that simple. To someone who already knew how to do it, it was *idiotically* simple, but for me, it was the difference between romping on the Web and being able to snap and save faithful pictures of what I found there. It was the difference between playing heedlessly and working purposefully. It was, in short, a revelation—the right information at the right time.

I could have gone to Google and typed in *save webpages* and received similar instructions, and perhaps had an equally profound epiphany, except that I didn't know that *saving web-pages* was what I was looking for. I didn't have the vocabulary to ask Google what it knew, or maybe I didn't have the vision: it never occurred to me that you could save, not just the content, but the whole page, including the flashing ads and links. That's the trouble with ignorance.

The librarian's kindness was a bonus. She hadn't laughed at me. If I had asked her how to make the little black mark in the middle of the screen move, she would have shown me how to use a mouse—and if you don't know how a mouse works, the person who shows you is a genius.

I thanked her for the help. My gratitude was appreciated, but she hadn't helped me as a favor. This was her *job*.

The Massachusetts Library Association developed a handy way to calculate the value of the services your public library provides. You estimate how many books you check out, how many newspapers you browse, how many hours you used the computer, and so on, and it puts a dollar value on those services and totes them up. According to this calculator, one question answered by the reference desk is worth $7. (Other states picked this up and use a version of the same formula, but value a reference question at $15.) But what if that question was hugely important to you? What if the answer affected your livelihood?

This testimonial appeared in *Feel-good Librarian*, a blog posted by an anonymous public librarian in the midwest United States. It appeared about a year into the economic downturn, soon after a tornado delivered another blow to the region:

> Literally thousands of people are out of work in our tri-county area.... These former factory workers, some with limited English language skills, and very few computer skills, must use the internet to file for unemployment, get entered in our state's required database and post a résumé. I consider myself fairly computer savvy and this is a cranky, confusing and unfriendly interface.
>
> Many of our patrons do not know how to type and do not understand why they need an email address, much less how to establish one. Taco Bell, McDonald's and Wal-Mart, as well as the larger employers in our area, all require applications to be filled out online. People who can't even speak English well are required to make résumés without knowing how to say the word ("my

rezoom" is how one patron referred to it), much less fill in the form with properly capitalized names. One man did not know what a capital letter was....

Good public libraries offer computer classes for both rank beginners and experienced researchers, and good librarians have been showing people how to use e-mail for years—but how to use capital letters?! So when I hear this snarky question (and I hear it everywhere): Are librarians obsolete in the Age of Google? all I can say is, are you kidding? Librarians are more important than ever. Google and Yahoo! and Bing and WolframAlpha can help you find answers to your questions, sometimes brilliantly; but if you don't know how to phrase those questions, no search engine can help provide the answers. It can't explain in simple language how e-mails (let alone the rules of capitalization!) work, or how to navigate government websites. You can only get so far without human help.

Google couldn't answer the question posed by a man who had been walking in the woods when he came across a stone plaque covered by strange marks. He copied out the marks and took them to the library, hoping to find out what they meant. Brian Herzog, who blogs as the *Swiss Army Librarian*, was working on the reference desk that day. He suspected his patron had stumbled upon a clue in geocaching, a kind of contemporary treasure hunt that uses GPS locaters. Where we'd see chicken scratches, Herzog saw an ancient language being used as a code in an outdoor game. Herzog's account of *his* hunt that day to determine what part this plaque played in the literal treasure hunt involved good hunches, multiple resources, deductive logic, and the creative application of advanced reference skills. Ultimately, he figured out that the marks spelled out, in runes, a number; when plugged into a GPS device, that number would lead to the next clue. This was a hunt with a real treasure at the end, though as searches go, it was an exercise in curiosity and not a matter of whether the patron's family would eat that night. Still—what price could you put on the professional who took up your whimsical search with enthusiasm and spent his day ensuring its success?

And how would you value the reference librarian who answered the question, "Where can I find a book on bootyism?"? Check Google for bootyism and you'll find out all you ever wanted to know about booty shaking; Google didn't prompt, as it occasionally does with presumptive misspellings, "Are you sure you don't mean . . . ?" But librarians are trained to prompt till they figure it out: Ah, not bootyism—Buddhism.

Mosman Library, located near Sydney, Australia, sponsored a contest involving two librarians, one armed with the library's online reference resources, the other with Google and the free Web. For five days running, they were given forty-five minutes to solve a challenging question—one was about alternative therapies for Parkinson's disease, another about women writers of the Beat Generation. I couldn't wait for the answers to be posted each day. There's something about the game-show format that sharpens the teeth and quickens the blood. No outcome could be as exciting as the race itself—the blink of the library's webpage as it refreshed and posted the updated results with the latest comments from their colleagues scorning Wikipedia or applauding the contestants' speed.

The librarian working the library's databases was more efficient, accurate, and concise (she could find great answers in two or three minutes) than the one surfing Google, although he had been very resourceful wading through the junk to find authoritative answers. But the moderator of the contest declined to declare a victor. "You," the patron, were the winner. And, yeah, we patrons *are* lucky; we get to use both the library's resources and the Web. For my money, though, the librarians themselves were the winners, skillful jockeys who could tear through tracks of all kinds of information and race back with the prize, the right answers.

In late 1996, the Benton Foundation and the Kellogg Foundation released a joint report titled *Buildings, Books, and Bytes* that questioned the value of librarians. Both foundations have been leaders in researching educational uses for media and the Internet, and this report was a valuable sounding, an effort to get a sense of what the public wanted from libraries.

. . . the focus group participants placed libraries at the fringes of modern life, especially in relation to the technological revolution. Most telling, they did not see libraries leading the way in the digital revolution. In fact, they thought libraries should take a reactive role, adapting to new technologies. Libraries "should stay just behind the curve. We don't need them to be on the curve because most people aren't," as one participant put it. Indeed, in a world of tight budgetary constraints, these Americans did not want to invest in libraries as technology leaders. . . .

When asked to think about the role of libraries in the future, they placed libraries firmly in the past. In 30 years, they said, libraries would be relegated to a "kind of museum where people can go and look up stuff from way back when."

The "public" the Benton report consulted were eleven white, middle-class, middle-aged people who described themselves as frequent library users. I'm guessing that these people had computers and cable television at home and lots of book and video stores nearby to provide entertainment and intellectual stimulation. To them, libraries were emblems of prestige, nice places to hang quilt shows; a library was like a pair of glasses their community wore to look smart.

The focus group participants . . . acknowledged that librarians could perform a useful role as navigators in the as-yet difficult-to-navigate universe of the Internet. Yet they just as easily sanctioned the notion that trained library professionals could be replaced with community volunteers, such as retirees.

It's all too easy to picture, as their long discussion came to a close, the focus group relishing the piling-on phase. They had whaled and walloped on libraries for hours; it was time to go home. Replace librarians with community volunteers? I could see him, the smug citizen, leaning in to lob the last brick: "What's the difference between a librarian and a retired volunteer? About $40,000."

The Benton and Kellogg researchers didn't accept the conclusion that people wanted nothing more from their libraries. After further research, they suggested that people were nostalgic for the libraries and the librarians of their youth. They were loathe to see librarians change, but as long as they didn't change too much, well, a little technology in their libraries might be all right. Librarians weren't all that enthusiastic, either, not at first. "They resisted Internet access—but it was the only service that took off without any advertising," in the words of one young librarian. The experience of the New York Public Library on Fifth Avenue was typical; there had been wifi in the periodicals room for years, but not in the reading rooms. No announcement had to be made when it was introduced there in 2007; within hours, everyone in the reading room was online. The wired library was inevitable. It was happening, whether people were ready for it or not. With Bill Gates seeding computers in libraries, and Al Gore pushing through legislation for federal funding for broadband access, the Benton Foundation prepared a briefing packet—and sample posters with slogans like "Surf the net, or dive into a great book"—to help librarians get out the message that there was room in libraries for both books and bytes.

Late in the 1990s, I saw my local public libraries shake off their dust and stir to life. The new hardware was a crucial component, but no, really it was the librarians themselves who were making the difference. They got computer training. They took charge of the machinery, the computers and printers and copiers that often broke down or ran empty and dry; they had a designated computer troubleshooter on staff, and teenage computer whizzes who came in after school to teach patrons and help the librarians. They bought computers through their consortium, which kept them serviced and updated them every few years. Instead of tearing their hair out about what *else* had landed on their plate, and what *else* could go wrong with the cursed machines, librarians added another responsibility to their set of jobs.

That spot behind the technological curve sucked, as anyone knew who had stared in frustration as impenetrable symbols cluttered the webpage, or watched his files disappear, or felt momentarily flummoxed when someone asked about his browser (*Which one is the browser?*). It felt like you were getting stupider. It felt like being trampled by horse hooves in the age of cars. And the experts, frankly, were obnoxious. How many times can you stand to hear variations on "You just don't get it." Really, it was simple: Where else could you go, who could you trust, what could you afford? For many of us, librarians are the best and sometimes the only answer.

That early focus group was wrong. Librarians need to be ahead of the curve. And it was their lucky day, and ours, too, when computers came to the library.

The silver-haired librarians who got their library degrees way back in the twentieth century came from backgrounds in history and literature. These days, it's more likely to be computer majors wending their way through information science school—people like Jenny Levine: "Hi, my name is Jenny, and I'll be your librarian today," she announces on her blog *The Shifted Librarian*. Levine happens to be in Chicago, but that doesn't matter. She lives on the Web, where anyone can find her. She has a following, built up over the years she wrote *Librarian du Jour*, a blog that sent those just learning how to use the social web off to explore new sites. Levine belongs to a new generation of librarians who proudly call themselves *geeks*. They pepper the Web with computer-savvy tools and techniques, and at every conference or gathering of librarians, Levine or her equivalent will be there to train, mentor, and troubleshoot. Welcome to Library 2.0, where librarians prowl the untidy streets of the Internet.

The annual American Library Association conference in 2007 featured 27,000 librarians pouring through the streets of Washington, D.C., descending on the Walter E. Washington Convention Center and filling every nearby conference room. There were multiple Library 2.0 sessions on the program, such as "Once Upon a Furl in a Podcast Long Ago: Using New Technologies to Support Library Instruction"—a sexy title for a librarian panel. It made my heart beat faster, because I knew about Furl (which has since morphed into Diigo), one of those free and ingenious bibliographic services that let you organize the articles you find online. The panel's organizers had miscalculated the turnout, no doubt thinking, "Furl . . . podcast . . . how cute!" and had scheduled the panel in one of the smaller hotel conference rooms. The crowd was double what the space could hold. I had to step over librarians young and old in the hall and the aisles, then pick my way back through the tunnel of a room to find a chair. *Of course* librarians showed up for a presentation on using the new technologies. They need to know.

The panelists, all academic librarians, presented a unified front. They agreed that computer users could be divided into digital immigrants (those of us who were trying to catch up) and digital natives (younger people seemingly born hardwired for the new technologies, or maybe it's just that they've studied computers in school). With the exception of a few very young, edgy-looking women, most of us in the room counted as immigrants—me and the silver-haired librarians. In spite of our best efforts, we were never going to master this language that those born after about 1980 speak so fluently. We could learn the lingo and tools of the digital age, but we would always have a thick accent when we spoke. We were babushka-wearers (I don't deny it; I'm sure I sound like Borat talking about computers). It was too late already to be whiz kids, though we could be trained. And, by the way, if any of us ever thought of teaching a class by standing in front of rows of students and lecturing, we should hop onto the back of the next sled and roll off at the nearest tundra. Because the digital natives did not learn by being lectured to. They learned by collaborating, networking,

sharing. They were not just consumers of information, literature, wisdom, history, all that good stuff—they saw themselves
as creators, too.

In one of those sweet stories that transcend the divide,
panelist Kathy Burnett remembered the class of library students she taught at Rutgers way back in 1990. It was a course
in introductory programming called "Internet Interfaces," and
as part of their exploration, the students—all of them women
over thirty-five—posted a notice on one of the early shared
spaces on the Web, asking for help. They found it in the form
of a knowledgeable guide who coached them online for ten
weeks. He turned out to be fourteen.

You never know what shape your information guru will
take.

I would not have pegged the fresh-faced young woman on
the panel as a guru, and I doubt she'd describe herself as
such; too modest. Neat, straight brown hair, and glasses, a
black suit over white blouse, she looked like part of an army
of young, smart preppies, her mouth often tilted with humor
or in a dry aside. Kathryn Shaughnessy of St. John's University
in Queens (New York) was jetting off to Rome in three days,
she said, to teach a class of twenty international students in
the university's new master's program in Global Development
and Social Justice. The students would be coming from India,
Palestine, Thailand, Africa, and the Caribbean, and speaking
English, their second or third language. Most of them would
be on scholarship; at least one of these students would walk

through the door and say, "Is that a computer? I've heard of these computers." It was Shaughnessy's job as an instructional librarian to give them enough information tools that they could return to their (certainly poor, possibly war-torn or disaster-trashed) home countries prepared to spend two years completing graduate school online. They weren't just learning for the sake of their own educational ambitions; the students would be researching conditions in their country, experimenting with activist solutions, and posting the results to the bank of world knowledge. They needed to know how to use these tools to help their communities. Shaughnessy had conducted this immersion training the year before, for the first class of master's candidates, and trying to keep the students all on track and online through the past year had been harrowing. But she and the program had survived, and now she was about to repeat the experience and double her responsibilities.

I'd never imagined a librarian missionary, or considered the concept of intellectual charity. And yet now, listening to Shaughnessy zip through a condensed version of her course for the benefit of the gathered librarians, my brain was doing cartwheels. The most important tool for the far-flung students was the RSS feed, the real simple syndication that brings to a single page all the sites you want to monitor. Why was that such a helpful tool? Because the computer didn't need to be turned on for an RSS page to be updated; the most current news was always waiting there, a plus when their access to power was limited. And this was no joke: one of her students had had to use his motorcycle battery for backup when the town generator blew.

If Shaughnessy could get someone who'd never seen a computer before up and running, capable of using Skype's free Internet telephone to talk with teachers and fellow students, monitoring world events through RSS feeds, posting statistics and photos on blogs and Flickr, making podcasts—in mere *weeks*—then wasn't there hope for us all?

3.

ON THE GROUND

This is the greatest and most fraught romance of modern society, the marriage between the IT staff and those who depend on them.

Martha Alcott, head of reference services at the Chappaqua Library in Westchester County, New York, called the information desk at the beginning of the migration, to see how things were going. What's a *migration*, you might wonder? It's an interesting word choice that summons up hordes of human refugees, or flocks of geese; but in this case it meant 4 million digital catalog entries were being transferred from one application to another, a move as fraught and risky in its own way as a dash across a six-lane highway. The Chappaqua Library was one of thirty-seven in the Westchester Library System, a consortium just north of New York City, all sharing the same software. It had been in use for eight years—an eternity in the world of computing. The consortium had been told that the catalog software was so old its vendor would no longer offer technical support. Ready or not, all thirty-seven of these networked libraries had to suffer this improvement.

The migration was happening even as I looked around the library, but such are the mysteries of progress that all seemed placid on a particularly sleepy Saturday in April 2007. A few people surfed the Internet, but the catalog-only computers sat blankly on desktops, corralled between the stacks and the sun-flooded reading room with its periodical displays, the *Wall Street Journal*, the *New York Review of Books*. Throughout the building, in patches of natural light, printed warning signs in stand-up Plexiglas frames declared: "Please be patient while we change our software! April 6th–April 16th. No more than five items checked out at a time! Patrons must have their library card to check out items—no exceptions!"

We were in the land of rules and exhortations. The rules weren't odious, but still—"no exceptions!"

Carolyn Reznick and Maryanne Eaton had been on the job since the place opened at nine a.m. The signs had had an effect: the usual crush of Saturday-morning traffic in this literate community had slowed to a trickle. This was a town of mothers with law degrees stashed in drawers, of people whose foreheads throbbed during the three-second wait at the cash machine. The idea of limits and delays, the prospect of librarians writing down titles, product codes, and library-card numbers by hand, had dampened enthusiasm for free DVD rentals. The only question being asked at the information desk was: "What's wrong with the catalog?" No matter how many times Reznick and Eaton repeated the sentence, "Our system is being upgraded," the librarians never rolled their eyes or got irritable, but instead smiled in welcome. "Can I help you? Our system is being upgraded. Thank you for your patience. Yes, the catalog will be down until the sixteenth. Thank you for your patience."

Reznick liked to call libraries "the new village green," but not today. She was prepared to help with Internet searches, government documents, reading suggestions, term papers, résumés—any of their information needs—but few were asking. "It's dead in here," she told Alcott, one reference librarian to another. "It's a tomb—which is good, because nothing is working."

Somewhere, the digital catalog was chugging and churning through a server, perhaps in Huntsville, Alabama, where the SirsiDynix Corporation has its headquarters, its numerous software engineers, and its computer troubleshooters.

And until the upgraded catalog was ready, library patrons who needed to find an item in this 450-square-mile county—whether they lived in one of the affluent suburbs like Chappaqua, a mixed economic neighborhood along the Hudson River like Tarrytown, or a rural stretch to the north like Somers—had to rely on their reference librarians, who had access only to their old internal databases, which "unfortunately during this time period . . . may not be accurate," according to the flyers. Westchester's towns had grown increasingly interdependent by way of this solid and useful library system, but for ten days the county would have to drop back to the olden days of, say, the late 1980s, when every town was an island and you had to use the old-fashioned telephone to borrow another library's book.

A Chappaqua mother, petite, fashionable, and grim, approached Reznick with her awkward teenage daughter. The daughter hung back while her mother explained that the girl had lost a book she borrowed from the library. The mother waved her hand at this annoyance—"That's not a problem, we'll pay for it"—but the girl needed another copy of the book for a paper due Monday. In fact, she needed the book *right now*. The mother would drive her daughter anywhere to get it. But where?

Reznick didn't blink or judge, even when the mother said the lost book was "not a problem." She looked up the title on the internal catalog, which indicated there was a copy on the shelf in Armonk, a few miles away. Then the system logged off. This logging-off business had been happening all morning and was driving her crazy; each time she had to reboot and use her password to get back in.

Reznick conducted the rest of the rescue mission by telephone. Yes, Armonk had the book and would hold it. Success! Volatile mother defused, daughter saved, and they didn't even have to drive to some sketchy or faraway corner of the county; they could go to the nice Armonk library, with its quaint historic photos lining the entrance and lots of parking space. The woman did not quite twist her daughter's ear and drag her out the glass door that slid open on their approach, but she left behind a trail of static.

The pleasant face that Reznick showed the public disappeared as she punched in the phone number for the information technology (IT) staff at the Westchester Library System headquarters in White Plains and got one of the computer guys on the line. "This isn't right, Wilson. The application is timing out every five minutes! Every time I look something up, it freezes. How can we do our job?"

Four million items in the Westchester Library System, separated from their catalog. It was the first day of the migration, and the stress had just begun.

A book I ordered about digital archives had arrived from outside the Westchester system via interlibrary loan—thrill!—so I settled in with it at the information desk with Reznick and Eaton. I was reading about sophisticated digital cataloging in an old-fashioned book with so many primitive paper records attached that both a paper clip and a rubber band were needed to secure them. Still, it was worth all the trouble a bucket brigade of librarians had taken to get it to me, full of juicy observations about this curious transition period we're living in and our rush to hit the delete button. I found a little perspective in one of the book's quotes, this from an Oregon newspaper: "The videotape of the first Super Bowl game was erased and NBC wiped out a decade's worth of Johnny Carson shows. Today, we wonder how TV executives could have been so stupid, even as we repeat the mistakes."

Between chapters, I chatted with Reznick (faux-leopard-skin flats, wheat-colored jean jacket, gray-blond layered hair). She had gone to graduate school in history at the University of Wisconsin back in the sixties and taught in Montreal, where she frequented a library in a shopping mall that was open 365 days a year from ten a.m. to ten p.m. "It served me well," she said fondly. When she couldn't find a teaching job after moving back to the States, she got a library degree. This was in 1992, when there were few computers and most library catalogs were still stored on cards. Reznick has no nostalgia for the old system. "I remember in grad school searching for a nineteenth-century book and trying to contact maybe Harvard or Indiana or Berlin to see if they had it." Now there was WorldCat, which could tell you in a nanosecond that all three had it, and so did the college up the road. The digital catalog, lightweight, almost invisible, and searchable without leaving her seat was "*infinitely* better." With the public librarian's pragmatism, she and the rest of the Chappaqua staff recycled the thousands of loose cards from the old catalog as scratch paper.

Reznick rarely bought books once she became a librarian; she borrowed most of what she read—history, mainly. But she remembered accumulating books in grad school. "Maybe some-one flunked out, but he tossed all his books into a Dumpster, and I crawled in and fished them out." Dumpster-diving for books! Those were the days! She had since mastered the book chaos in her home, another benefit of becoming a librarian.

Almost every day one of her patrons tried to reverse the flow of books by donating a box of discards to the library. Officially, though, there were only two days a year the library accepted used books for the annual book sale. On those days, the park-ing lot was jammed with SUVs and station wagons, while vol-unteers unloaded grocery bags and liquor boxes full of Erma

Bombeck, Arthur Hailey, James Michener, Herman Hesse, Carlos Castaneda. In this town, you were not doing the library a favor by donating books. *It* did *you* a favor taking them. But when an older man staggered in the first day of the migration with a box of moldering paperbacks, the librarians on duty took pity. Eaton carried the box in and picked through the spoils. "Here's a book on the Easter uprising for you, Carolyn. And a whole bunch of Graham Greenes."

I love Graham Greene, I admitted. Eaton wrinkled her nose. "But they *smell*!" We all laughed. Somehow the Graham Greenes ended up in the back of my car. They did smell, all the way home, but I couldn't dump these great novels from the fifties, with retro graphics and yellowed pages. They were Graham Greenes, for crying out loud, work by a great writer whose world-weariness and seedy sentiment somehow suited the packaging. Besides, I could use a little trick an archivist taught me—a sheet of Bounce would absorb the musty odor.

It was a different sort of migration than the one taking place with our digital records; this was the timeless migration of books, those antique delivery systems, moving through the library and into my hands.

I ran into one of the reference librarians at a local coffee shop, or maybe it was at the movie house that plays artsy foreign films, the one where the sophisticated librarians hang out. I didn't know her name, but she'd helped me more than once. I had to greet her. "There's that famous librarian!" I said. She laughed. "There's that famous patron!"

By now I know most of their names. I first met Gwen and Deb and Carolyn and Martha through my children. The librarians' faces light up when I walk in; they're *my* librarians. I visited them frequently in the weeks after the migration, and each time, they seemed a little more frazzled. "How's it going?" I'd ask, and their pleasant masks would drop and they'd show me another face—hassled and frustrated. The day before the new software debuted, all hell broke loose. The winds and rain of the worst nor'easter in years blew through the eastern seaboard. It was one thing to be experiencing a maelstrom in cyberspace, but ridiculous to have a literal maelstrom on top of it. Seven and a half inches of rain—flooding in six of the Westchester libraries—electricity out, roads closed, National Guard out in force. Did I really need to ask how they were doing?

When the catalog finally went online—"the longest eleven days of my life," according to Chappaqua's director—it was "buggy." The location of this library's children's collection, according to the new catalog, was "unknown." Two days later, the whole thing crashed. Poor librarians! Weeks later, the system still didn't work the way it should. One librarian confided: "There are no answers for us. There was a meeting, and the liaison person was saying robotically after every question, 'We're working on it. We're working on it.'"

"Unfortunately, the move has been disastrous," a memo from the Westchester Library System admitted to its member libraries. There was an underlying problem with the database. The system couldn't generate overdue notices, leaving the libraries armless, without the capacity to recall their overdue books; and the catalog had to be "re-indexed," whatever that meant. Title searches of the catalog came back full of junk. I entered the title of my last book, *The Dead Beat,* and the first hit on the search list was a CD from Psychopathic Records by the Insane Clown Posse. And the *holds,* those precious waiting lists that determined who would get the next copy of the new bestseller or DVD release, sometimes disappeared. When? Seemingly at random. Why? They had no idea. And librarians aren't programmed to say, "We have no idea." The words feel like chalk in their mouth.

Who was in charge of these computers, anyway?

This is the greatest and most fraught romance of modern society, the marriage between the IT staff and those who depend on them. You see it in offices, where a measure of power has shifted to the tech departments, to the people who can unfreeze your screen, unlock your files, link you to the world you have to be linked to; you see it in the Apple Store, where men and women sit humbly and gratefully on stools while boys and girls in "Genius" T-shirts show them how their computers work.

You can also see conflicted variations of this model playing out here, between the librarians on the ground, who worked the computers, and the IT department that serviced them. It didn't matter how tech-savvy the librarians were; during the migration they were helpless to do anything but complain. And the IT staff trying to diagnose and fix the problems were being driven crazy by their complaints. It was a culture clash rooted in that imbalance of power, and it was being dramatized daily in Westchester in the spring and summer of 2007. The librarians were at the mercy of the IT department, and the IT department was at the mercy of the software. And all of it was landing on the desk of Wayne Hay, the head of IT.

Like most information professionals, Hay was a font of facts. He could figure out where to find the best of anything—gadgets, pepperoni pizza, schnitzel—and he had been at it a while; now in his late fifties, Hay was a teen computer programmer when he started working part-time in libraries. He looks like Santa Claus, complete with white beard and belly, though in his usual outfit of jeans and a sky-blue polo shirt, he's more Santa-as-beachcomber. "I'm no spring chicken," he admitted, "but I do my homework." If his schmoozy style of talking, love of Brits and their television programming, and passion for miniature dachshunds (he has four) signal a certain style, this was complicated by his Columbus, Ohio, roots. Hay's other passion, for Buckeye football, bordered on mania; the pen on his desk played the Ohio State fight song. Every hour or so, in his shirtsleeves, he left his office and ducked out to the loading dock to smoke a Carlton, whatever the weather.

Hay was the first person I knew to buy a Kindle, which he immediately began using to read the *New York Times*. He pushed downloadable audiobooks to the librarians and touted Playaways—preloaded single-book audio players. He described himself as being in "the bells-and-whistles department." But he also believed that "Putting books into people's hands is our number-one service. Don't talk to me about reference," and he quoted a 2002 study from OCLC that said people used their libraries mainly to check out books, not to get information. High-tech, low-tech, either, both—just get them the books and DVDs.

He was friendly with librarians across the country as well as in his consortium, and a librarian himself, but his assessment of them as a group was harsh. "They're their own worst enemy," he said. "They should have to work retail for a year! I don't want to do things through technology for the benefit of the *librarian*. I want to benefit the *patron*. Library 2.0 is user-centric—it's not about what makes the librarian's life better. Just because librarians like to search for author, title, subject the way they used to in the old card catalog doesn't mean the general public does that anymore. The card catalog is dead, people. Move on." It's a keyword world now.

He made no apologies for his bluntness. A decade ago, Hay had met a legislative aide while lobbying for the federal government's E-rate program, which helped reimburse libraries and schools for their broadband access. On his way out the door, she told him, "Wayne, librarians have to be louder." He'd taken the advice.

During the early part of the migration, Hay stayed in a hotel near his office to cut his two-hour-a-day commute and worked late into the night; one of the Sirsi engineers pulled an all-nighter to work around a problem. For a whole day, the nine people on the IT staff retyped records that had been incorrectly coded—by the librarians, Hay pointed out. But these efforts were slow to bring results. Meanwhile, the librarians on the ground were trying to accustom themselves to a Windows-based system after years of more ancient DOS-based computing, but the training they were getting from the vendor, Sirsi, was proving inadequate. "Banging your head on a wall would have gotten you further," as one IT guy put it. Hay's efforts to keep the branch libraries informed about the problems and delays seemed to backfire, often revealing his exasperation with the librarians. ("It would help if we do not get calls asking for status every few minutes.") One librarian printed out copies of his e-mails and saved them in a binder she called "Adventures in Sirsi-land," a bitter souvenir.

Behind closed doors, Hay admitted he would like to shoot all librarians over twenty-five. Or maybe just all librarians. (Their adjustment to the new system, he noticed, coincided with the summer influx of student employees.)

Besides the training shortcomings and the messy catalog entries some of the libraries had fed them, SirsiDynix and the consortium's IT department had taken turns screwing up. "Big deal," Hay said. "That's what happens when you do this sort of thing, and everyone has to get over it. What—do you think this is magic?"

Their choices had been limited; library vendors were all consolidating, and only three of them could serve such a complex consortium. Everyone, librarians included, had agreed on the choice of Sirsi. But "library search engines are old, old tech, old architecture," Hay explained. "We're now at least twelve years past the revolution in the nineties that led us to Google and Amazon, and the vendors are still hitting us with structures that frankly date back to the seventies. Library automation needs new software big time." Westchester was stuck for the moment with its vendor, but within months of the migration, Hay's staff was researching alternatives—open-source software that the IT department would help write and adapt. In the next phase of library history, librarians won't simply provide access to computers and use them to catalog, communicate, and network—they'll write the programs as well.

But technostress continued to infect Westchester's library system long after the spring migration had ended. "It was bad; it was so bad," said Chappaqua's director, Pam Thornton, "I thought about pulling my library out of the consortium." The executive director gave Hay a withering performance review and referred to 2007 as "the year of hell." And there was a lingering technical problem: random holds from the list of patrons waiting their turn for the hot books and DVDs were still disappearing, which baffled both the IT guys and the Sirsi technicians. None of them could target the problem.

Hay traveled all over to stay on top of technology and keep the Westchester libraries up to date. "It's an investment. Why attend conferences in Europe? The last ten hot products came from Europe." He first heard about RFID tags—radio frequency identification devices that can be implanted in books, or anything else—at a European conference, way back when, and was able to persuade one of the directors in his consortium, then building a state-of-the-art library, to invest. Now whole stacks of books and DVDs could be checked in or out in seconds, without opening the covers or searching for the bar codes, making self-checkout possible and misshelved books and DVDs a problem of the past.

The British Library was Hay's touchstone. He admired its use of technology, its website, and its braggadocio: "10,000 pages on our website." He appreciated the way the director was called the "chief executive officer." I suspect he would have loved to work there. Hay had discovered a nifty feature on the British Library's website, called Turning the Pages; this was an interactive digital program that let you flip through Mozart's notebooks while listening to his music. "I want to fall asleep when people talk about digital content, but this is digitization in a fabulous, user-friendly manner. You can actually read his music in his handwriting." He longed for one of these toys for Westchester, and imagined using it to animate an old history of the county.

Hay was at a library conference in Oslo, standing outside the convention center, smoking and chatting with a woman who was raving about her library: it had a machine she could visit at any hour of the day or night. "Oh, tell me more," Hay said, whipping out his pad. "And then I walked inside and there was this machine. Now that's a concept!"

Hay described it as "a small automated library branch—in a box. It's robotic on the inside, uses RFID, the radio frequency tags, all robotic arms, and you can borrow books and DVDs from it." Hay began talking with the two Swedish owners about the possibility of importing five of the machines, called Bokomaten ("book machine" in Swedish) for a test run in Westchester.

We were in a corporate park in White Plains, sitting in his little office, piled high with books, DVDs, manuals, and the remnants of a pepperoni pizza. He had a Dell computer behind his desk linked to a smaller monitor that faced me. "See?" Hay said, clicking on a YouTube video he posted from the Bokomaten's marketers. The machine rumbled to life, operated by disembodied hands, as a narrator spoke in lilting, Swedish-accented English. Hay said: "I've been talking up the ATM for books ever since I got back. I keep saying, 'Guys, this is your chance to go first. Think of the publicity!' But they'd just as soon go second."

Hay and his staff, frustrated by all the money the consortium allocates for databases that relatively few patrons use, and fleeting investments like public relations, were trying to shift expectations and priorities. They prepared a presentation for the consortium's administrators and board members called "Rethinking the Library," a video tour of cutting-edge libraries in Scandinavia, Europe, the U.K., and California. One of them, called Ideastore, had been cropping up in East London; it was the flip side of the British Library—a blend of community centers and circulating libraries that had room for continuing-education classes, media centers, and cafés. I visited one in London and found it to be a hive of activity in a tough neighborhood, the "village green" writ in concrete. *Look at all you can do here!* was the message patrons got when they walked into one of these places. Instead of putting up signs that read *no cell phones*, for instance, like most of the libraries I frequent, the DOK Library Concept Center in Delft, Netherlands, invited patrons to bring their cell phones, park them in their special docks, and load them up with free content: music, film trailers, college lectures. The librarians there bragged, "If there is a Library 2.0, then DOK will be 3.0."

"They're into it. And we don't get it," said Hay.

Almost a year after the migration, Hay reported to the library board that a number of the catalog issues that bedeviled the system, including the inexplicably vanishing holds, could not be blamed on technology. "In many cases, these issues were traced back to personnel/input problems and not direct system problems," he said. There was a little explosive charge behind his carefully chosen words. The holds were not mysteriously disappearing because the Sirsi system screwed up and the IT department failed to diagnose the problem, and they didn't stem from innocent user error or inadequate training. Rather, it seemed, a few librarians had been going into the computerized hold queues and deleting requests, moving their own names up the waiting list to claim the hot items for themselves.

The sweethearts of free culture, the helpmates of the mind, this selfless profession turned out to harbor individuals who couldn't wait their turn to consume *Dewey: The Small-Town Library Cat Who Touched the World*. Or was it the BBC version of *Sense and Sensibility* that drove them mad with longing, mad enough to forget their ethical principles and vows to serve the public? Whatever it was, the desire for it had thrown a low-tech wrench into the system's $787,000 catalog.

My smart, conscientious, friendly librarians slammed the

drawer on those grasping fingers that had uncharacteristically crept out from behind the circulation desk. The furious directors disciplined the perps and drew up a document articulating their ethical expectations for every library employee, including the high school pages, the book shelvers. I never did learn what constituted discipline for renegade librarians, though I didn't spot anybody with brands or burns or dislocated thumbs. More than any group I can think of, librarians are identified with their profession, and the laughs and jeers don't stop when some stickler tries to collect a dead person's fine. So this transgression was dealt with quietly. It was all I could do to get one of the directors to confirm it. "Most of us are honest," she began, before admitting that, "yes, a couple librarians were jumping their relatives ahead of other holds for new DVDs. And everyone thought we had a software bug, and was blaming the IT guys."

Hay shrugged it off; he didn't want to discuss it. His two deputies shook their heads. Their competence had been called into question, but what can you do? This migration had been a perfect storm of screwups.

For nearly a year, I had struggled whenever the librarians tried to explain their circulation challenges, or the IT people tried to explain the need for reindexing, the "junk" they said librarians had thrown in "the volume fields" that messed up the searches, beating my head against the language of libraries and computers. But here was a culprit I understood. I ran home and danced around the table, singing, "Guess what! You know the screwed-up catalog? The one driving everyone nuts? You know what caused the last bug? Greedy librarians!" Obviously, the stress had affected me, too.

Of course most librarians are honest; that's one reason it took so long to figure out what was wrong. The point is, libraries that share an IT department share a nerve center, and few can afford to stand alone these days. A little action in one place radiates through the whole system.

And let's put it in perspective. In 2009, the New York Public Library merged the separate catalogs of its research and circulating libraries—eight million records all together—into one. Harried librarians there were coping with irate patrons, lost holds, and checkout lines that snaked out the library doors. A librarian observing the disruption summed it up: "There is no such thing as a smooth conversion."

But back in 2007, the Westchester librarian just trying to do her job pulled out her "Adventures in Sirsi-land" binder, full of memos from headquarters wishing her a "Happy Gloomy Morning" or exhorting her to "smile a lot and forgive fines." She wanted the online catalog to work, that's all. Why couldn't the IT department make that happen? And what was with Hay? "Look," she said, "he actually wrote, 'I'm going to have a cigarette to calm down.' Do you believe that?"

Was he taunting her? It was almost as if they were *married*, and divorce was in the air.

And in a sense they *were* married, the librarians and the IT department—for better or worse, for richer or poorer . . . in technological trauma or robust cyber health.

4.

THE BLOG PEOPLE

*Is it any wonder the whispering behind the library
staff doors has turned into exclamations on the
Internet? They can't keep this stuff to themselves.*

They *seemed* to be quiet types, the women and men in rubber-soled shoes. Their favorite word, after *literacy,* was *privacy*—for their patrons and themselves. They disappeared into their staff rooms and we heard . . . nothing—no buzz of gossip, no shrieks of laughter. We didn't even hear the squeaks from their shoes.

Library science has always been a discreet profession. Have you ever had a librarian confide her pain or personal heartache while on the job? Not likely. Once I asked a reference librarian of the slightly chilly ilk where to find the graphic novels. I was looking for a copy of *Maus.* "Oh!" she said, her face lighting up. "I love that book." (Someday, I will stop being surprised at all the things librarians read; they'll read anything.) Then she took me to the rumpled teen corner of the library, found *Maus*, and placed it in my hands with a blessing. "I hope you love it, too." I looked back on decades of patronage and realized that this was the most a librarian had ever revealed about herself in a professional exchange.

Librarians were the last people I'd expect to make noise on a social network. And yet, in the last decade or so, librarians took to blogging with a vengeance. Blogs turned out to be a natural medium for these inveterate browsers and bibliographers to post their links. They were useful catch-alls for sharing reviews and discoveries. They were places to reflect on your work and speculate about the future, to gossip and rant. You could swear freely and anonymously on the Internet; the wilder your personality and the more scathing your satire, the more readers you attracted. Unedited and unmonitored, blogs represented a kind of free expression that librarians traditionally supported and celebrated, but had rarely taken the opportunity to practice.

The computers that carried the libraries' catalogs and linked them to the Internet were also do-it-yourself publishing centers. With the rise of easy-to-use blogging software, free hosting sites, and a built-in readership—colleagues conscientiously paying attention to the new medium and looking for sites to visit on the Web—people didn't need programming skills to reach an audience. They simply needed things to say, and librarians, as it happens, were cauldrons of previously unexpressed passions.

There are upward of 150,000 librarians in this country, so

the stampede to blogging had an impact. "They are multiplying like rabbits," librarian Rory Litwin wrote in 2002 in a bit
of a panic over the proliferation of the "Wild Librarian" websites. Lists of the Top Ten Librarian Blogs morphed into the
Top Fifty, and barely scratched the surface at that. Most of the
writers were talking to each other, but since they were talking
on the World Wide Web, there was nothing to stop outsiders
from reading and laughing over their shoulders, picking up hot
information and technology tips. It was easy to eavesdrop on
the librarians.

The ranting, mocking model prevailed. "Why you should
get on your knees and worship a librarian" was the banner on
the Librarian Avenger's home page, but it could have served for
most of them. Every possible distinguishing feature attached
itself to the title Librarian and marked a blog home on the
Web. Bunless, Depraved, Disorganized, Eclectic, Foxy, Gypsy,
and Lipstick Librarians joined Free Range, Scattered, and
Shifted Librarians in the *biblioblogosphere*, as librarians called
their corner of the Web. And then there were the librarian
bloggers who let off steam that seemed to have built up since
the Steam Age: *The Annoyed Librarian*, *The Effing Librarian*,
Librarian's Rant, *Miss Information*, *The Obnoxious Librarian
from Hades*, *Shhhh!!*, and, with a mission explicitly articulated
to document the assholic behavior of patrons, supervisors, and
coworkers, the baddest-named blog of all, *The Society for Librarians Who Say Motherfucker*. Yes, there were librarians who
called their patrons *mofos* behind their backs. The Dutch librarian Dennie Heye created an obnoxious librarian alter-ego

to vent and entertain; his *Obnoxious Librarian from Hades*, who longed for the days when librarians used to chain books to the stacks, called library users "lusers." (And this guy had been named the European Special Library Association's 2008 Information Professional of the Year.)

There were straight blogs that spread news about a library's services, acquisitions, and events, and blogs that did the same job with attitude, like *Pimp My Library*. The 2.0 librarian bloggers wrote about the intersection of libraries and technology and beat the drum for networked information and technical literacy: *Info Babe, InfoFetishist, Information Wants to Be Free*. In less than a decade, this silent profession turned clamorous. Open, casual, approachable, dedicated to demystifying technology and networked to the eyeballs, the bloggers became the public face of the twenty-first-century librarian. And the "blog people," as library leader and occasional grump Michael Gorman scornfully called them, became the celebrities of the librarian world.

Seriously

People serious about the future of librarianship and their role in it launched serious blogs, minus the effing-studded posts. Some attended a workshop called "Blogging for Professional Development"—and *then* they started blogs. The drumbeat urging librarians to blog came in the form of cheerful encouragement ("having a blog shows you have a constructive online presence. . . . A blog is also a good thing to list on your business card. . . . It feels great to be part of the community . . . sharing ideas and promoting the field"—advice from *The Inspired Library School Student*) as well as short, free, do-it-yourself courses, developed by smart librarians and posted for their colleagues (or anyone) to learn the new tools of the social web.

Young, eager computer geeks took their first steps into the library profession by blogging. "So, how did I become a librarian?" wrote Lichen Rancourt, a tech whiz in her thirties. "Is it too smoochy to say I think I always was one? My mom is a librarian . . . I loved computers; it just kind of made sense." She attended an information science conference in 2005 and was struck by lightning. "Jenny and Michael opened doors that day for me. I came home and started a blog."

Everybody is first-name familiar in blogland. Fortunately, I had read enough librarian posts to know immediately which Jenny and Michael she was referring to, though Lichen helpfully linked both names to their websites. There were several semifamous librarians named Michael, but this one was young ponytailed Michael Stephens, an assistant professor at Dominican University in Illinois whose blog *Tame the Web* blended technological savvy and human enthusiasm. Jenny was Jenny Levine, one of the earliest of the librarian bloggers and a proponent of gaming in libraries. (At conferences, Jenny would set up a stand in the lobby and show librarians how to play tennis on the Wii. The first thing I saw, arriving at more than one library convention, was the laid-back Jenny and a couple of librarians whacking at the air in front of their gaming screens.)

The ALA hired Jenny in 2006, and she has been developing digital initiatives. Now she has lit another beacon on the frontier: her ALA CONNECT, a social network for librarians, lets the profession communicate and collaborate and keep records of their committee meetings in one online hive.

I pictured the dynamic, motormouth Michael prowling the stage, the laconic, rumpled Jenny clicking the mouse and flashing pictures on the screen behind him, both wearing jeans and flannel shirts, putting the tools of the trade into Lichen's hands with encouraging smiles. They were dream recruiters for library school. Almost anyone who spent time skipping around librarian blogs or attending conventions would know about these two engaging proponents of Library 2.0. Many would also know Lichen, who had been fomenting technological revolution since that fateful day at the conference; she has since earned her library degree and gone on to direct technology at the Mansfield City Library in New Hampshire and also write experimental software.

Dip into any of the serious 2.0 librarian blogs and you'll fall into this network of smart, young, articulate coders and catalogers, with the temperament to wade into the rough-and-tumble Internet and a mission to light a path through the maze. In *Remaining Relevant*, for instance, Lichen linked her two inspirations, the conference that changed her life (complete with podcasts of Jenny and Michael's presentations) and the online university and degree program she subsequently enrolled in. You could follow in Lichen's footsteps, and if you, too, were inspired, she made it easy for you to instantly register for library school. Or the excellent *Librarian in Black* ("resources and discussions for the 'tech-librarian-by-default' among us") would lead you to sites like LibraryThing, where you could become your own librarian and create an electronic record of your own books and music. Too much trouble to enter the titles by hand? *Free Range Librarian* reviewed Library-Thing's fifteen-dollar scanner, which swept over your books and cataloged them automatically. Librarians, in short, were swarming the Web, exploring and mapping it, while linking readers to the shiny, or useful, or fascinating things they found along the way.

P.S. Don't worry about that *smoochy* in Lichen's post. Lichen Rancourt was hardly the mushy type—"Curse the shoddy wifi," she tweeted during one library conference; "how is this a problem at every single conference? Network peeps, is it really that hard?"—so her post "Is it too smoochy to say I think I always was [a librarian]?" should be read with a wink. Yes, librarians used punctuation marks to make little emoticons, smiley and frowny faces in their correspondence, but if there were one for an ironic wink, or a sarcastic lip curl, they'd wear it out.

One of the goals of Library 2.0 was to bridge the distance between the expert librarians and us, the public. Blogs made librarians accessible from anywhere. We could follow them virtually into their staff rooms; we could even follow them home. Michael Stephens wrote his Ph.D. dissertation about blogging librarians; that's how much he believed in their power to disseminate information and create community. Occasionally, he admitted, his exposure on the Web seemed to invite a sort of creepy familiarity. In *Tame the Web*, he recalled the night a strange young woman called him via video-chat, in the hope that, because he had written about his Mac, he could help fix hers (he tried, unsuccessfully). On another occasion, he wrote, "I was floating on my floatie in the middle of Spider Lake on a HOT day when two kayaks approach. 'Hello,' says the younger of the two fellows. . . . 'Are you the guy that has all the pictures up on the web of Balsam Circle?' 'Yes,' I say, glancing around and feeling suddenly vulnerable. 'I googled Balsam Circle and Spider Lake and found all your pictures. We wanted to FIND YOU.'" They were stalkers, but benign ones. "We chitchat when they pass by in the mornings now," Michael reported.

This was certainly a different kind of librarian from the ones planted behind the reference desk. Michael was in a bathing suit—on a *floatie*—his labeled pictures out there on the Web where anyone could find them. This willingness to be found, not just online but also out in the field, in his own pond, took a certain amount of courage and faith in the good intentions of his public.

Jessamyn West started her blog, *librarian.net*, back in 1997 as a way to keep her mom informed about what she was doing, and from the start she was an open book, generously posting about nine different ways readers could contact her directly. She linked her professional blog with her personal blog, *jessamyn.com*, where she actually gave the world directions to her home in Vermont. "Pretty much everyone's welcome, with some notice, including decently behaved pets and kids," she declared. "The place is hell on the allergic, bring your meds. . . . I cannot stress enough that there is nothing to do out here in many conventional senses. Please come prepared to amuse yourself, or amuse me. . . . It always helps to bring food, beer or board games. If you are here more than three days, I'll put you to work." Personally, I found it hard to fathom this openness—I freaked when I learned Google maps linked directions to my house with my address—but the combination of blunt honesty and post-hippie friendliness suited Jessamyn's style as a librarian and personified the open Web.

It also gave those of us with questions another place to go. If our neighborhood librarians were off duty, we could always find Michael or Jessamyn or one of the other librarians floating on the Web. Or we could consult the online resources they had assembled, like the program "Five Weeks to a Social Library" launched by five tech-savvy librarians, which brought me up to speed on wikis and Flickr, or Jessamyn's homemade video called "Ubuntu @ the Library." This was a Keystone Kops–style romp set to a spirited Cajun number, showing Jessamyn installing, with ease, the Ubuntu open-source operating system on an old computer donated to one of the rural Vermont libraries where she works. At some point Jessamyn brought her adorable face up close to the camera and chatted while waiting for the system to load on the old computer. Then she showed us all the games and other features before the BeauSoleil soundtrack propelled her into a happy closing frenzy. The YouTube iteration of her video was viewed well over 100,000 times. That's stardom in the library world, and inspiration, too; how many old computers have been revived because of her example?

K. G. (Karen) Schneider calls herself "the world's oldest millennial"—she's barely fifty, but most of the bloggers and geek librarians are at least one decade, if not three decades, younger. Since 2003, she has been posting high-tech commentary, news about her literary work, and dispatches on daily life with her cats and the woman she refers to as "mrs. kgs" on her blog, *Free Range Librarian*. Her prose has a real voice, breezily familiar, even playful. "If you want to do one thing for me, your favorite gay person (I am your favorite, right?) please view and share *Prop 8: The Musical* starring Jack Black." Like the rest of the 2.0 librarians, she traveled frequently from her home in Tallahassee to speak at library conferences, and published her personal schedule so people could locate her, even when she was offstage: "1:30—4 Exhibits (walking with a friend)," she detailed, or "11:00 p.m. ALA Midwinter After Hours, Moriarty's Irish Pub . . . (tentative—that's awfully late)."

I caught her after a panel discussion called "Do Libraries Innovate?" (not enough yet, she and the other experts, all blogging librarians, agreed), and trotted with her from the hotel venue on to her next event at the Washington, D.C., convention center. An ALA staffer—"our Sherpa," Karen teased— guided us along the crowded summer sidewalks.

She mentioned, small world, both Michael Stephens (she'd

helped with his dissertation), and Jessamyn West, whose video had just rocketed through the blogosphere. "She makes a great representative librarian," Karen said. "Bloggers are more iconoclastic than most librarians, as you might have noticed. It may not be one hundred percent representative of the profession, but it's a good image."

While power-walking, Karen reflected: "Maybe I'm just feeling optimistic because I'm at a conference, but basic library literacy has reached a tipping point." She didn't mean literacy as in reading books—of course librarians can read! She meant *computer* literacy. "If you don't do the technology by now, you're either retired or you're off in a corner, waiting to be retired. There is still too much tolerance in the profession for being uncomfortable with technology, but not the way there was when I started fifteen years ago."

Karen is tiny, not quite five feet, and moved on that hot afternoon with speed and efficiency. "You know, she used to fix F-16s?" our guide said. Karen confirmed this; she had been a maintenance officer in the Air Force, where "lack of innovation was a deterrent to your career—and so was lack of excellence." She quoted another blogging librarian, who had said, wryly, "Only in our profession would people who consider e-mail annoying be allowed to serve on a committee for tech innovation." The librarians' desire to extend their hand to all and their "Quakerly love of consensus," as one put it—not to mention the relatively slow turnover in the ranks of elders—worked against streamlined innovation and took a toll on progress, at least as measured by the high-tech crowd. To Karen, librarians needed to step it up.

She helped launch the American Library Association's blog *Tech Source*, and for two years, she prodded and hectored librarians to use the tools of the web and rethink the profession. Her personal blog was her current "bully pulpit." She sensed its impact almost immediately. Her literary work could take years to publish, her essays on technical topics, weeks; but she could blog about something on *Free Range Librarian*, and it would say, "Posted 2 sec ago." Half the fun was in getting comments and continuing the dialogue; to subscribe to a blog without subscribing to its comments was to miss part of the point. "It's the most amazing way to network with the world," Karen enthused. And, just to give it a librarian spin, she added, "I love it that you're self-archiving in real time."

Lest you imagine that all is smoochy in library blogland, let me point out that librarians, known for their tolerance and insistence on equality, can also be quarrelsome and fractious.

The anonymous *Annoyed Librarian* ("Whatever it is, I'm against it") calls Jenny, Michael, Lichen, Karen, and the crowd they run with the "twopointopians" (2.0 + utopians). Annoyed has made it her particular mission to belittle the new wave of techie-librarians and cast suspicion on their motives; they've made careers out of showing librarians what librarians could easily, she claims, find out for themselves. And their enthusiasm galls her: "'What an exciting time it is to be a librarian! How lucky we all are! What great fun we all have! What wonderful opportunities we all have! How exciting it is to bc us!' Do any of us really get excited by all the supposedly excited librarians around us? Or do we just wonder what meds they're on?"

Her pointed, mocking, funny posts on the *Annoyed Librarian* are as widely read as any of the upbeat, tech-savvy posts on *Shifted Librarian* or *Tame the Web* or *Free Range Librarian*. When *Library Journal* began hosting her anonymous blog, the outcry was immediate. Who *is* Annoyed? Even the *Library Journal* editors claim not to know and negotiate with her (or him) through lawyers.

As for the benefits of a networked profession, video-gaming in libraries, Twitter, or anything else that hints of hipness—don't make her laugh. Annoyed is into ridiculing the profession and amusing herself and others while she nibbles "vermouth-soaked olives." As for blogging? Annoyed sneers, "It ain't that hard. Even I have a blog."

The Real Poop

I had no idea poop was such a problem for librarians. Each day—and when I'm really into it, that means twelve times each day—I go to my RSS feed and scan the ninety-seven librarian blogs I monitor for new posts. (I'm a lightweight; Sarah Houghton Jan, who gives a goth twist to information science on her blog, *Librarian in Black*, keeps up with 450 of them.) I can always count on a dozen or two of these bloggers to enlighten and amuse me on the topic of technology and libraries, which is saying something. Kathryn Greenhill, a sharp Australian with the blog *Librarians Matter*, for instance, posted no fewer than six videos of librarians around the world performing variations on Michael Jackson's *Thriller* (with book carts and without; with zombie makeup and without— fascinating and kind of scary). Kathryn, like the other 2.0 bloggers, is engaged in an occasionally playful but mostly serious effort to fast-forward librarians into the future. She isn't blogging about the mess behind the stacks.

Happyville Library was not a blog about poop, but poop was its genesis. It began in mid-2005 as *Libraries for Dummies*, but a certain publishing concern felt it owned the word *dummies*. So the writer came up with the name *Happyville Library* for her blog. The Happy Villain, as she calls herself, takes great pleasure in documenting the deranged goings-on in the public library in Illinois where she works. I remember a long, lovingly written post about checking in a DVD with goo in its slipcase. "What's worse? White goo or brown goo?" she mused. "I'm struggling right now with that question." Finally she decided, "Goo is never good." Another post consisted entirely of "signs we never thought we'd need to make," each of which told its own condensed story:

While waiting for your ride home, do not set fire to your homework to keep warm.

You may not take the *Sports Illustrated* Swimsuit Issue into the washroom.

Iguanas are not allowed in the building.

**If you are out of diapers, do not open the soiled
diaper, scoop out the turd, leave the turd on
a shelf, and then ask the librarian to tape the
newly cleaned diaper closed again. . . .**

She wrote about her coworkers, too, until one of them
made a formal complaint. In order to keep her job, the Happy
Villain agreed to shut down the *Happyville* blog and never
write another negative word about her library, its patrons, or
her colleagues. The only *Happyville Library* post that can be accessed on the Web now is the last, her farewell to the world of
library blogs, with dozens of comments trailing below, some
of them howls of disappointment: "I don't think I can live in
a world in which the Happyville Library blog does not exist.
You're killing me here!" and "No, you can't leave! I need your
blog too much for you to go!! You always show me that I'm
not alone in Library Weirdo Land," and, most tellingly, "I have
always enjoyed how you can write so well about poop."

Did you ever? I mean, did you *ever think* that being a librarian meant dealing with poop? Talking about it, finding little
piles of it in the stacks, writing about it on the Web. I certainly
never thought that *I* would have to write about it. In fact, one
of the things that appealed to me about this book was the intellectual, cerebral, almost disembodied nature of the subject
of librarians in the digital age. I envisioned leaving the physical world altogether and leaning into the computer screen to

commune with my subjects—following them along the path of digitization and the vapor trails of their thoughts, leaving even the mild stink of old books and rotting newspapers in the dust. I imagined the wired world of information and literature, full of brilliant, helpful, visionary librarians, as gleaming and immaculate as an Apple Store, except not just for those who could afford the Apple merchandise. I was spending my life trying to focus on what was new in librarianship: new attitudes, new targets for outreach, the new issues and possibilities that computers in libraries represented. I didn't want to be sitting in a sticky chair thinking about poop. Children, the homeless, smuggled-in soda bottles that spill all over the stacks, poop—these were all problems, as the academics would say, beyond the scope of my inquiry.

And yet, here was poop.

Kristen Gilbert, who works in a library in Rhode Island and blogs as *Crissy, Queen of Fucking Everything*, reports that her coworkers were abuzz the day they discovered someone pooped in the book drop. There was much speculation about how exactly the deed had been accomplished—perhaps the guilty party had pooped and then deposited it, since the alternative, given the construction of the drop, would seem to make balancing during the act difficult. Crissy thought it hilarious, but the librarians she worked with did not. I asked other librarians. Yes, poop is a problem, though not as big a problem as slashed budgets, the high cost of electronic databases, and the preposterous fees OCLC charges libraries to use

WorldCat. However, one librarian recalled a patron they used to call Sir Poops-a-lot, who left a trail of turds in his wake.

I wrote to the Happy Villain (whose e-mail address included the phrase "goo is never good"), hoping to gain access to the *Happyville Library* archive, but she continues to live in fear of losing her job, which, she hastened to point out, she likes. "I've heard many stories about anonymous bloggers who were 'outed' and lost their jobs, and frankly, I just cannot risk it." As for the poop question, "Yes," she told me, "people have left poop in the most unbelievable places. Mostly down in the youth department, but we have found what I have dubbed 'rogue turds' all over the library. What amazes me is that other librarians e-mail me routinely and say they too find them and are somewhat comforted to know that it's not just *their* patrons doing this, but everyone's. . . . People from faraway places like England, Japan, New Zealand, and Australia let me know that it happens there as well. People are strange creatures."

Rogue turds! Is it any wonder the whispering behind library staff doors has turned into exclamations on the Internet? They can't keep this stuff to themselves. "When I first started blogging," Happy Villain continued, "there was a terrible backlash from more prim and proper folks in the field, who butchered me on the Internet for disgracing their profession by making fun of some of the situations I found myself in. It wasn't even that they didn't like my sarcasm or my scathing retelling of events. These people were angry that I had violated some code of silence that said we weren't supposed to talk about our 'bad' patrons or 'geeky' coworkers. . . . Despite how far it's come, the field still abhors a big mouth."

She admitted that her personal blog, *If I Ran the Universe*, scoured as it is of most sarcasm and complaints, didn't quite satisfy her. "I really miss the old days because there isn't much catharsis out there for me anymore."

The Happy Villain watches other bloggers write about the absurd and abundant material in libraryland with envy, while her unvented observations gather steam. The pressure gets to her. Recently, she was writing about a conversation with another librarian on the subject of "the weirdos in our field." Before she knew it, she had exploded: ". . . we forget how normal and stable we are until we attend a meeting at the consortium, and when these freaks return to the Mother Ship, all the stops are pulled out. I would not be surprised to find anyone wearing aluminum foil helmets or devouring their own young. . . ."

After we corresponded for a while, the Happy Villain confessed: "I did start another blog in the same vein as the old one, 100% anonymous, but I don't update it often because I'm too paranoid that my bosses are out looking for me to start a new one. . . . Writers seldom just stop writing. We're like serial killers in that way. You have to stop us, because we cannot stop ourselves."

5.

BIG BROTHER AND
THE HOLDOUT COMPANY

*"The basic thing—what we held on to—was,
it just isn't right to do this to innocent people."*

The PEN America gala was just like high school, except instead of a prom king and queen, we had a tuxedoed Salman Rushdie and Padma Lakshmi in a slinky gown, gathering her skirts and melting into the revolving door at the Museum of Natural History. If you want to stand with the angels against censorship and fatwas, the PEN gala is an inspiring event, and a scene, as well. Famous literary types in sparkling evening wear gather to cheer the courage of writers and others who had risked imprisonment and worse to tell their truths. Inside the museum, the great hall of ocean life was lit like an underwater cave. A massive blue whale hung over the scene and flocks of seabirds and walruses behind glass witnessed our splendid invasion. And somewhere in the program, between the announcement of the winner of one prize and another, a modest-looking man and woman from Connecticut were asked to stand and take a bow. The FBI had sent them and two of their colleagues a national security letter, a top-secret demand to hand over their libraries' computer records. Rather than comply, the Connecticut Four challenged the USA Patriot Act that authorized the letter and sued the government. They had been gagged, essentially, for a year while the case worked its way through the courts. Now they were free to be recognized by name and honored for defending our right to privacy and freedom from unreasonable searches and seizures. Three librarians and the director of their library consortium, collectively known in the court case as "John Doe," had become, arguably, the most celebrated incognito heroes since Deep Throat. George Christian, the director, and one of the librarians, Janet Nocek, now stood and waved and smiled at the enthusiastic applause. Christian's glasses winked in the spotlight.

My husband and I clapped and cheered along with everyone else, but we were also laughing. Unknowingly, we'd been standing with Nocek and Christian at the reception earlier in the evening, making small talk that began when the man had excused himself, leaned over to my husband, and plucked a piece of the dry cleaner's cellophane from his tux. We thought we were passing the cocktail hour with two other wallflowers, lucky enough to score a ticket to this cosmopolitan scene. Instead, our fellow nobodies turned out to be the whole point of the PEN gala. We had been standing with our heroes.

A few weeks later, I drove up to Hartford to get John Doe's story from Christian and Nocek and their colleagues, Peter Chase and Barbara Bailey. A spring nor'easter was pounding the East Coast with rain so hard I hydroplaned up Interstate 95. What was a few inches of rain and some fierce, almost 50-mph winds compared to defying the FBI? This happened to be the same nor'easter that was at that very moment flooding Westchester, the first of the series of blows that challenged that county's networked libraries. Here the storm led us to another story of networked libraries—but this one featured a consortium where the tech people and the librarians were firm allies, operating together so harmoniously, they were able to put a wrench in the secret workings of the federal government.

Let it also be noted that these people came from their far-flung towns in a biblical downpour to sit in the café of the Mark Twain Museum in Hartford and recount their stories for me all afternoon, as if they had never told them before, had no other pressing business, and weren't soaking wet. Having been gagged, they felt a duty to speak out and explain themselves to anyone who wanted to hear. They had made history, as their obituaries would someday record. They didn't have the option to be nice, quiet librarians anymore.

I commandeered a corner table near a big picture window, behind which an old oak tree was doing battle with the storm. I wiped the table myself, so I knew it was crumb-free when George Christian sat down and plucked an invisible mote off its surface, just as he had plucked the scrap of cellophane from my husband's suit. A fastidious man. The Mark Twain Museum was central for the scattered librarians, and symbolic, a monument to one of Connecticut's great literary figures, a writer who stood firmly against sheeplike behavior in human beings. "It is our nature to conform; it is a force which not many can successfully resist," Mark Twain once wrote. I was sure his spirit would be with us.

Few principles rouse librarians more than the right of free access to information and the right to privacy in our choices. If a librarian phones our house to say a book we've requested has arrived, she will not tell our husband that *Confronting the Batterer* is in; she won't tell our children we can pick up that copy of *How to Break Bad News*. What we searched for on library computers, from information about cancer or trans-sexuality to instructions on how to build a pipe bomb, was our own business. As recently as the 1980s, the FBI urged librarians to report people with Eastern European–sounding accents or names who were looking at scientific material; they called it the FBI Library Awareness Program, and librarians en masse resisted it. There are library confidentiality laws in place in forty-eight U.S. states, and rulings favorable to library confidentiality in the other two (Hawaii and Kentucky), and policies had been developed at most libraries to guard against "unreasonable searches and seizures"—everybody remembered that amendment, but librarians had developed muscles defending it. If an agent of the government wanted to know what we'd been reading, he had to show "probable cause, supported by Oath or affirmation," or a good librarian would stand between our records and his badge.

The dance between library privacy and the government's desire or need to know is complicated during war, but passage of the Patriot Act in 2001 alarmed many librarians. Was the FBI now going to help itself to library records, with or without search warrants? No, no, Attorney General John Ashcroft declared, and Alberto Gonzales after him; no one wanted your library records, and no one's civil liberties were going to be violated. Librarians who implied otherwise were simply being, as Ashcroft put it, "hysterical."

Then, in 2005, George Christian and Library Connection, a consortium in Connecticut that furnished computer services to twenty-seven member libraries, received a national security letter from the FBI demanding information about who had used one of their computers on a particular day. It was a matter of national security, the letter said, but no judge had signed it—and Christian was warned never to reveal the letter's contents, or even acknowledge having received it.

The letter hadn't completely surprised him, George Christian recalled at our meeting. Someone from the FBI had called Library Connection's telecommunications manager and asked to whom they should address a national security letter; they had been given Christian's name. Tipped off, Christian first thought, "I'd never heard those three words—'national security letter'—together before in my life."

Neither had his attorney, who did a quick survey and learned

of a challenge then wending its way through the courts. It was
initiated by (who else?) "John Doe," this Doe an Internet service provider in New York who had refused to comply with
his national security letter and was suing to have it declared
unconstitutional. The judge had ruled that "on its face, the
statute violates the First, the Fourth and the Fifth Amendments." The government was appealing, but Christian was
encouraged. "Not one amendment—three!" Obviously, he
had a case. Section 215, the part of the Patriot Act that authorized the use of secret national security letters to gather
books, records, papers, documents, and other items "in connection with" a terror investigation—without judicial review
and oversight—had to be unconstitutional.

The FBI agents didn't appear at Library Connection's door
immediately. When they did, the letter was months old and
the information the FBI wanted dated back five months.
Christian had no desire to aid and abet terrorists, but the
agents didn't seem to be in "hot pursuit. I didn't think that I
was putting anybody at risk if I stalled on this." He told his
attorney he didn't want to comply with the letter. And she told
him there was only one alternative: he would have to sue the
attorney general.

Legally, Christian had the right as executive director of
the consortium to file on his own, "but morally I didn't feel
I could commit the consortium to a contest like this. I could
just see this going to the Supreme Court and the bills running
up like crazy." He decided to bring in the other members of the
executive board, three library directors—Nocek, Chase, and

Bailey—who had just been elected to their posts. Once they saw the letter, they, too, became subject to the gag.

From the start, there was no question they'd refuse to comply with the FBI. Retelling their story in Hartford that afternoon, they sounded like an echo chamber.

Nocek: "Oh, not going to do it."

Bailey: "We're not going to do it, no."

Chase: "We're not gonna do it, not without a court order."

Nocek: "Not without a court order."

Chase: "I couldn't believe there was no court order. I said, 'What do you mean there's no court order?' How can they ask?"

Nocek: "I remember shaking a little afterwards and saying, 'Geez, we could be abetting terrorists.' That came to mind. The basic thing—what we held on to—was, it just isn't right to do this to innocent people."

Chase: "People come to libraries and they tell us very confidential things all the time. 'I'm sick. I have cancer. Where are the medical books? I'm thinking about a divorce. Where are the legal books?' They trust us with that information, so we're not going to sell them out. People want to read different opinions, different views. Maybe they're reading Osama bin Laden because they want to find out what it's all about. So spying on what they're doing in the library, we always say, is like spying on the voting booth. This is where people can make up their minds about controversial issues. It *has* to be private."

They were like a chorus, voices chiming in, then fading as

one soloist, then another, stepped forward. I looked around the table at these middle-aged, unobtrusively dressed citizens, who fell effortlessly into the background until they opened their mouths and spoke. Who were they?

George Christian, mustached and tall, had a slight stoop even while seated, as if bending down to listen to his companions. Though he was the leader of the "Connecticut Librarians," as they came to be called, he was not a librarian. Hired to manage Library Connection's computer system and deal with its vendors ("because I wouldn't succumb to the song and dance that vendors give"), he was a tech guy so attuned to the librarians that he ended up running the consortium.

Barbara Bailey would have been a Spanish teacher but for a glut in the market. She had bright blue eyes and short blond-gray hair she raked with her hands. She was the director of the Wells-Turner Memorial Library in Glastonbury; she called herself "a small-town librarian."

Jan Nocek was very young when she "got hooked" working in libraries. Her first was in Salem, Massachusetts, home of the infamous witch hunts. "Of course," she pointed out, "we're naturally suspicious of accusations and judicial [overreach] there. Terrible things can come of that." Another small-town librarian, she directs the Portland, Connecticut, library.

Peter Chase was once a history teacher. He spent a summer working on a bookmobile, then switched enthusiastically to library work. As director of the Plainville Public Library and chairman of the Intellectual Freedom Committee of Connecticut, he was outspoken about the dangers of the Patriot Act.

Chase had publicly debated U.S. Attorney Kevin O'Connor, who ended up their adversary in court, on the subject. "O'Connor continued making forays throughout the state to promote the Patriot Act, and I would be asked to go to some of those events, too, but of course I couldn't accept, nor could I explain why I wasn't accepting," he said. "It was galling for me to see him travel around, telling people that their library records were safe, while at the same time he was enforcing a gag order preventing me from telling people that their library records were *not* safe."

But the hardest part for Chase and Christian, both fathers, was concealing their activities from their almost grown children. They wanted to explain that they were not doing something wrong—they were standing up for their principles, the Constitution of the United States, and every American who lives under its protection—but they couldn't do that without risking jail.

The American Civil Liberties Union agreed to represent the plaintiffs, a tremendous relief. But after the ACLU filed suit in federal court in Bridgeport, Connecticut, to halt the search of their libraries' computers and get a ruling on the constitutionality of national security letters, Christian and the three librarians' cloak-and-dagger days as John Doe (Connecticut) began.

Christian: "The attorneys said, 'We really don't think you should use the phone that much, or e-mail.' I thought that they were being a little dramatic. They collected the copies of the national security letter I had passed out and they said, 'We think you ought to shred this. And if you're going to keep notes, do you have a locked filing cabinet? Really, you can't have this stuff lying on your desk. Somebody might see it.' "

Nocek: "It was ridiculous. I was called in for jury duty and they said, 'Are you involved in a suit?' They want to know what it is and I can't tell them. I didn't know what to do—I was under oath. I said I was involved, nothing else, and luckily wasn't called."

Christian: "I had to lie to our auditors. I'm the executive director and the one question the auditors asked me was, 'Is Library Connection involved in any serious legal matters?' And I had to say no, although I was suing the attorney general of United States."

Chase: "You can't go to a secret meeting with the ACLU in New York City and say to your wife, 'I'm sorry, I'm not going to Plainville, Connecticut; I'm going to New York City today.' "

Nocek: "Yeah, I'm running this library in a town of nine thousand—and I'm taking off for New York City every two weeks."

Chase: "Of course, my wife saw it all in the paper. It was pretty easy to figure out. Suddenly I had gone to the city and then there's a big headline the next day" (*FBI, Using Patriot Act, Demands Library's Records*).

They were not permitted in the federal courthouse in Bridgeport where their case, *Doe v. Gonzales,* was filed; they watched the proceedings on a closed-circuit television from

Hartford, sixty miles away. Bailey recalled: "We needed to pass through two levels of security and sit in a locked room with a security officer. We were plaintiffs, but we were treated like criminals."

A host of other Connecticut librarians, alarmed by the implications of the act, had shown up in Bridgeport, but Chase, the chairman of the state's Intellectual Freedom Committee, wasn't among them, and his absence in particular was conspicuous. Librarians, skilled at ferreting out information, had figured out that John Doe (Connecticut) had to be associated with Library Connection; now others were figuring it out as well. The *New York Times* reporter covering the case left her card in Christian's mailbox and called Chase at home. Chase told her nobody was talking about the case. The reporter wasn't fooled. She said to him, "The person *most* not talking about it is John Doe himself."

Chase had to report this conversation to the ACLU attorneys. They reacted with dead silence, then hung up for a hasty conference. " 'Peter, your situation has changed a little bit,' " Chase was told when they called back. " 'You've created a trace between your house and the *New York Times*, and if tomorrow's story identifies you as John Doe, people might get the wrong idea if they pulled your phone records, which of course they can. And so we've hired for you a team of criminal defense attorneys.'

"Luckily that news article didn't say my name, so the crisis was averted. But I think that really put the fear of God in me, how serious this could be. You had to be absolutely like a sphinx or you could be in trouble."

The Connecticut Four were permitted to attend the next hearing in the Court of Appeals of the Second Circuit in Manhattan, "but we could not enter the building together," Chase said. "We could not sit together. We could not speak to each other. We were not to look at each other."

Nocek: "Or the attorneys!"

Chase: "Or our attorneys. And because they had combined our case with John Doe (New York), we knew that someplace in that courtroom was John Doe (New York), our bosom buddy. But of course, he was under the same orders that we were."

Peter Chase was sitting next to the president of the Connecticut Library Association, who stood up and began ticking off the names of the other librarians who were pouring through the doors of the courthouse; in this way she hoped to signal to him how much support he had. When George Christian walked in, Chase recalls, "She said, 'Oh, look Peter, there's Geor——.' Then she sat down. She was afraid to say his name. That's what it was like . . . people were quite literally afraid to say our names."

While the government's appeal was being heard, debate over the renewal of the Patriot Act had begun. The head of the House Judiciary Committee stated, baldly: "Zero. That's the number of substantiated USA Patriot Act civil-liberties violations. Extensive congressional oversight found no violations." The attorney general released statistics showing that zero libraries or bookstores had been served with the national security letters. Meanwhile, the librarians who could contradict this claim were gagged.

The situation grew even more surreal when the *New York Times* noted that "even as the federal government was arguing in court that it needed to keep Library Connection's name secret, it had carelessly left its name sprinkled throughout court records." The Connecticut Four had been inadvertently outed by the government. The names of the Library Connection, George Christian, and Peter Chase were published in the *New York Times*, identified as plaintiffs.

Chase: "Our attorneys filed an emergency plea that said, 'Look, their names have been in the paper. Certainly you can remove the gag now because it's not too late for them to participate in the debate over the Patriot Act.' And the government said no. One of the arguments in its legal draft was that not too many people in Connecticut read the *New York Times*—and people who read newspapers, they don't believe what they read anyway. So really, the government concluded, their identity is still a secret."

What the four insisted on calling the "gag order" was officially termed the "nondisclosure provision." This rankled the librarians, too.

Nocek: "I could see a nondisclosure, where we wouldn't give away something that would jeopardize the investigation. But for nobody to be able to say they *ever* received one of these things throughout their whole life . . . ?"

Chase: "And to threaten you if you talk? That's a gag. I mean, English is English. That's how they lie with words. They pick the most innocuous-sounding terms."

Nocek: "It's absurd."

Christian: "That's why this is so *1984*."

Nocek: "I just found that totally reprehensible."

Christian: "Redefining words. And the very idea of a Patriot Act—it's not a Patriot Act, it's an assault on the Constitution."

The ACLU filed an emergency appeal to the Supreme Court, but Ruth Bader Ginsburg reviewed it and determined there was still plenty of time for the Appellate Court to make a decision; she wouldn't step on their toes. But time *did* run out. The Patriot Act was reauthorized in March 2006, with only minor changes. The government's assertion that not one national security letter had been issued to libraries went unchallenged.

Six weeks later, the attorney general's office dropped the nondisclosure order. The librarians were no longer gagged, but there would be no ruling from the Appeals Court on the constitutionality of such gags, and of course, it was too late to influence the debate on the Patriot Act. Being permitted to speak out after Congress had voted to reauthorize the act was, as Christian put it, "like being allowed to call the fire department after the building has burned down."

But once ungagged, the librarians had a few sharply worded things to say, and they said them to anyone who would listen: Do you know what the government is doing in the name of patriotism? It is asking for records that we assume are private; it is asking for them secretly; it is gagging librarians who try to defend that privacy; it is stifling public debate. And, by the way, is this the best use of our government agencies, in wartime and under threat of terrorism—sending out hundreds of thousands of secret national security letters, especially when any evidence obtained will be inadmissible in court?

So here was the case in a nutshell: quiet librarians who wanted to keep quiet about their patrons' records were told to give up those records and to remain silent about it. The librarians fought to be heard, and finally they were. Now, for the rest of their lives, they would be noisy, in defense of keeping quiet.

A few weeks after the four were finally free to speak, the government claimed it had obtained the information it originally requested by other means. Kevin O'Connor spoke publicly about the case afterward. As Chase recalled, "People in the audience were saying, 'Well, how come you didn't get a court order?' O'Connor said, 'We couldn't get an order because it wasn't a criminal affair.' He said it was a matter of domestic surveillance."

Christian added: "He said someone had used a computer at one of our libraries to inform the FBI about an alleged terrorist plot, and they wanted to talk to this individual. If it is now FBI policy that, if they get an anonymous tip, they'll move heaven and earth to find out who that person is, how many more anonymous tips do you think they'll get?"

USA Today later reported that the original tip had been a hoax.

"And of course, the whole thing was, we didn't have the name in our possession anywhere," Nocek said. Members of the Library Connection consortium don't verify the names of patrons who use their computers, and they don't keep the sign-up sheets for the computers for more than a few weeks. Also, they used a program that randomly assigned each machine a different Internet address every time it was turned on.

The FBI had asked them for information that didn't exist.

The national security letter addressed to Library Connection is, so far, the only one to become public.

Nocek, Chase, and Bailey are still directing their public libraries, and Chase continues to serve on the board of the consortium; Christian remains Library Connection's executive director. But much of their individual and collective time has been spent speaking out about privacy and government intrusion, or testifying, as Christian did, to the Senate Judiciary Committee; or as the former head of the American Library Association summed it up: "graciously agreeing to accept every speaking opportunity offered them, using each speech as a teachable moment and precious chance to inform [us] . . . about how far-reaching the powers granted in the Patriot Act are and how dangerous they are to the future of our democracy."

Chase said, "As librarians, we've been mass producers of information and distributors of information for many, many hundreds of years. And we've had a long time to think about honing those arguments on privacy." Their ACLU counsel, Ann Beeson, spoke of the case as a validation of their profession. "Congress won't follow laws, the president won't follow laws, the FBI won't follow laws, but we still have our librarians," she said.

The Connecticut Four have been honored with multiple awards, which came with their own challenges. At one point during our meeting in Hartford they veered into a conversation about an award that came with a monetary prize, and they were still trying to work out the technical details of passing the money on to their library boards. Nocek said she could live without reporters asking to follow her home. "One of them wanted to ride the train home with us after a press conference," she said. "I wanted to say, 'That's enough for now!'" But the attention was welcomed by Christian and Chase, the fathers who had lied to their sons for a year. Christian said that one organization honoring him had offered to fly his son to the ceremony, too, news that delighted the librarians. Dad wasn't a criminal, after all. On the contrary, he had been defending the Constitution.

The storm had quieted. The lunch crowd at the Mark Twain Museum had long scattered, but Christian wanted to explain something important before he and the others went back to work. "When the Patriot Act came out, librarians were very concerned. There are all kinds of provisions that came with gag orders." Christian had educated himself on the subject, attended legal seminars, met with other library consortia in Connecticut, and talked with them about jointly hiring a lawyer who could advise their member libraries on policy. "But then Attorney General Ashcroft said librarians were being hysterical; the Patriot Act has never been and never will be used against libraries. So we all went on to other things.

"But I had learned [from all those meetings] that you have to have a policy that whoever is in charge is the only one who can authorize the release of information. Everybody at Library Connection understood that if anybody came in the door asking for information, the answer was, 'I can't help you; you have to talk to the executive director.' If we hadn't gone through this drill, government agents could show up on a Sunday afternoon or Friday night or whatever. It's the FBI. They talk to some low-level minion. They flash their fancy badges and say, 'Look, it's national security; you've really got to help us out here.' Who's not going to say, 'Of course I'll help you out; what do you need?' And then after you give them the information, they say, 'Oh, by the way, you can't tell anybody we were here.'"

I thought of Rosa Parks, who had not been the first person of color to refuse to sit in the back of the bus but the first who refused to sit in the back and was also able to mount a long legal challenge. "You were prepared," I said.

"We were prepared."

They had planned for the knock on the door. They had drilled as if for a fire. They had centralized the usual bureaucracy of libraries and library consortia in case they needed to act, and when the time came, they had been ready for the challenge to the privacy of their patrons. It wasn't rhetoric. It was nuts-and-bolts and books-and-bytes teamwork.

What happened to the Connecticut Four occurred during the Bush era. But that couldn't happen again—or could it? The law authorizing secret searches by the FBI, unchecked by judicial oversight, extended until the last day of 2009 and has the support of the current attorney general, Eric Holder. The Safe and Secure America Act of 2009, introduced in the House in the spring, proposes extending this intelligence-gathering tool for another decade. The law is not going away. How many of our library records have been seized? The Office of the Inspector General estimated that more than 143,000 national security letters were issued between 2003 and 2005, but cautioned that these statistics "significantly understated" the actual amount. Chances are very good that your library use has been scrutinized by the FBI.

During the height of the debate about the Patriot Act, some librarians posted signs that were "technically legal," slyly warning patrons that their privacy might be compromised:

THE FBI HAS NOT BEEN HERE
(watch very closely for the removal of this sign)

There is no registry of libraries that have posted such signs, so there's no telling how many have since been removed. The reauthorization of the Patriot Act explicitly permits those who receive national security letters to consult a lawyer. It also explicitly adds a criminal penalty for "unauthorized disclosures." Librarians who post those warning signs now risk a five-year prison term.

6.

HOW TO CHANGE THE WORLD

Imagine activists around the world, wired to each
other and to the world's information resources,
each capable of measuring the impact of drought,
or tracking the efficacy of a prenatal clinic....

Almost everything about the scene was old-fashioned, even ancient. The setting was Rome, which sits on ruins. The librarians at the heart of it shared traditional values; one had a background in medieval philosophy. The principles at work were thousands of years old, rooted in charity. In fact, in almost all ways but one, these librarians inhabited an older and timeless world. But their mission had a quintessentially modern twist. They were teaching the others in their community how to video chat; how to post photos to Flickr; how to use GIS, geographic information systems; how to zip around the Internet; how to bend their laptops to the cause of social justice around the world.

Ever since I'd heard Kathy Shaughnessy, the librarian from St. John's, speak at the American Library Association convention about her cyber-missionary work teaching computer skills to students from a wide variety of countries, I had been eager to see her and her team in action, in Rome, where St. John's had a campus.

Shaughnessy's mother was a high school librarian who was fascinated by computers and convinced they could be useful in libraries. Under her influence, Kathy, the youngest of seven, studied logic and programming, and turned into the sort of person who couldn't wait to test the new software. After completing coursework for a Ph.D. in medieval philosophy, she moved on to her mother's profession. A "cradle Catholic," she measured her work by standards of social justice. "I like to look at the world and see how it is, and how it can be—how it *could* be—a little bit better if it was better organized. And the ability to access information and the ability to use computers—I see *not* being able to do those things as an injustice."

Shaughnessy's computer skills and philosophical background made her a good fit on the St. John's library faculty. She worked closely with the vice provost for distance learning and director of the Division of Library and Information Science, a visionary who was building the infrastructure for a university without geographic limits. In the nine years Jeffery Olson had been working on distance learning for St. John's, students had gone from not being able to pay fees or register online to being able to get a degree while living in Rwanda or India. (The university had also, incidentally, been named one of *PC Magazine*'s top twenty wired campuses in 2006.) Olson's team was equipped to launch this program before it had even been conceived.

Now Olson, Shaughnessy, an assistant professor and instructional services librarian, and Kevin Rioux, an assistant professor in the library school, were about to dispense laptop computers and digital cameras to their third class of international students, some of whom had never touched a computer. The job of the St. John's library team was to teach the students what they needed to know technologically, create an activist community across language barriers and time zones, then send them home, where the students would complete their master's degrees online over the next two years, write their theses, and, oh yeah, save the world.

I had been to Rome before—a pagan Rome, littered with half-excavated archaeological sites and crisscrossed by sleek women in high heels on Vespas. The Rome I saw this time, following Shaughnessy, was a company town, Catholic to its core. To get there, you left the urban heart, its fountains and cafés, the pines and palms and the crumbling walls of the old city, even the ancient bejeweled churches, and took the good subway, the air-conditioned one that rumbled beneath the city and emerged over the Tiber River, the Vatican glinting just long enough for a wave goodbye before the metro chariot plunged back underground and sped you nearly to the end of the line. One steep escalator after another pulled you from the center of the earth into a city drained of charm and beauty, a big

traffic corridor, no shade, vendors selling cheap purses, bat-
teries, baby clothes, and in the distance, a McDonald's, the
landmark where you turned onto via Aurelia and headed west
toward the Idente residence, a missionary training facility that
served as home base for the St. John's master's students.

I walked for half an hour in the Mediterranean sun, past car
dealers and gas stations and mysterious institutional buildings,
the only pedestrian lurching along the commercial thorough-
fare—whiz! honk! whonnnnnk!—barely a word of Italian in
my quiver, the least likely pilgrim on the planet. Shaughnessy,
in a flowered skirt and radiant smile, welcomed my limp and
bedraggled self into the placid interior of the building, where
long pale-green vertical blinds kept the atmosphere cool and
hushed. There were austere dorms upstairs, a cafeteria downstairs, classrooms and an open lounge with polished granite
floors on the main level—and free wifi throughout. The students walked around shyly, nodding and smiling, the Indian
women, the Caribbean men, most in their thirties and early
forties. Many of them were already nuns and priests, missionaries and human rights workers; this program would wire
them and give them a scholarly foundation. The newest class
was immersing itself in information resources, economics, and
theology classes, all of it in English, though most spoke multiple languages. The first class had reunited after two years
of staying in touch by computer. They were now winding up
their studies and preparing to graduate.

A vending machine dispensed perfectly fine cappuccino for
half a euro, so I sat and sipped and watched the students swirl

past as Shaughnessy pointed out some of the members of the Social Justice team. Sister Margaret John Kelly, tall and austere, in plain white shirt and dark skirt, a cropped veil hiding her trim gray hair, turned the corner with Dr. Annalisa Saccá, who was petite and dramatically made-up. A contessa with jewels on almost every finger, Saccá wore heels and a swirly skirt, her hands and face in constant motion. Two styles of women, one goal.

As Saccá told me later, she and her dear old friend Dr. Riccardo Colasanti, the secretary general of the Catholic charity Caritas of Rome, were having dinner one evening in the city, and Colasanti was confiding his frustrations. Caritas was pouring tons of money into charity, but as far as he could tell, it wasn't making much of a difference.

"How? How?" Saccá demanded, painted eyes flashing and red nails fluttering. "How can we change the world? Really!"

"We must find a new way of educating people!" Colasanti declared. So the two created an initiative on the spot: a graduate program designed to give people around the world some useful tools for promoting social justice: a program that would enable students to remain in their communities while learning how to investigate, document, and fight injustice using the Internet. Imagine activists around the world, wired to each other and to the world's information resources, each capable of measuring the impact of drought, or tracking the efficacy of a prenatal clinic . . .

Colasanti would provide the financial backing through his charities, and Saccá would rope in St. John's, which had established a presence in Rome. They chose "an empty box," an interdisciplinary master's program with flexible requirements—a master's in Liberal Arts with a Concentration in Global Development and Social Justice. Not "development" as in bringing McDonald's and Monsanto to your village; development in the sense of "realizing the fullness of human life." The key to implementing the program was the St. John's librarians and library school faculty, who would teach the students everything they needed to know to be long-distance students, keep them connected, and establish an online community for them. Saccá worked quickly ("She does everything quickly," Shaughnessy said) to win accreditation, and within a year and a half of her brainstorming dinner with Colasanti, the new master's program was recruiting students. Fifteen students, most from emerging countries, received full scholarships each year, including travel to and from Rome for their initial training, and again two years later, for their final presentations and graduation. Five students from the United States helped subsidize the program by paying full tuition and expenses, though one shouldered graduate assistant duties in exchange for reduced fees. The program would be technologically sophisticated, but Olson, a tall, smiling man with a gentle manner, stressed that the technological component was "not the end but an important means." The mission was the point; ThinkPads just happened to be efficient networking and delivery systems.

Every class I sat in on in Rome included a reference to Saint Vincent, the patron saint of the university and its affiliated priests and nuns. Vincent de Paul, a seventeenth-century priest, was a fine model for activists today, so the students were told. He was an advocate for women, slaves, beggars—anyone who suffered discrimination. Vincent believed in free will, equality, and dignity; he was also, according to Sister Margaret John, an organizational genius, a man who could figure out how to get people to support each other in simple but meaningful ways, such as helping a sick family by assigning their neighbors different nights to bring food. "And that's what we need now," Sister Margaret John said. "People who are really good organizers."

It sounded like they were all back-to-basics Catholics with laptops, a humanist message, and a special appeal to women.

"I'm not Catholic," Olson pointed out. "I'm Mormon."

Whatever they were, everyone dropped his or her work at lunchtime and trooped to the cafeteria, though, as Shaughnessy said, "It's much better than a cafeteria. It's Italy!" No one skipped a chance to break bread together, to share prosciutto and pasta, wine and grapes, the ancient repast.

In a city of thieves—as the guidebooks always emphasized—we all left our laptops, purses, and backpacks on a table by the door, and didn't give them another thought. The relaxed attention that everyone brought to the conversation, as well as the delicious food, was in civilized contrast to the tourist bustle in Rome proper. I asked Olson at lunch where I could read a history of the program, but he said it hadn't been written. "It's a concern to this profession—some of us are so worried about what is getting lost in this era—and we need to do more," he admitted. Just then a photographer arrived from New York to capture the first graduating class in Social Justice on film. At least there would be a photographic record.

That afternoon, the graduates posed for their portraits in the open lounge. The students slipped up to the dormitory rooms to swap their T-shirts and jeans and sandals for dress clothes. The Filipino and Indonesian men wore the traditional shirts made of pineapple fronds, called barongs. Four young women in vividly colored saris turned a little shy as onlookers exclaimed over their beauty. An African student was resplendent in her bright-red American-style suit. No one passing by failed to stop and compliment them, or offer hugs, or ask if any of their relatives had been able to come for the occasion. One young man's huge Italian-American family from Brooklyn would make up for those students with no one. A St. John's faculty adviser came from the U.S., though he had no classes to teach in Rome. He had mentored two of the students and simply wanted to see them graduate.

Not everyone who started the program had made it. But Eugenie Murekatete, who lost her husband in the fighting in Rwanda and was now working at the UN, was graduating; Parnel Saint-Hilaire from Haiti, who had just become a father, and whose baby cooed through more than one presentation that week, was graduating; the Vincentian activist from Indonesia who had kept them all posted during protests, the two men who had disappeared from the online community for weeks after a typhoon in the Philippines—they were graduating, and others, too, a dozen in all.

The first two classes had had audiences with Pope Benedict XVI while they were undergoing their initiation in Rome, further evidence of the religious pull of the program's founders, Saccá and Colasanti, but he was out of town this year, so the newest class of students missed out. They did get to attend a UN conference, sponsored by FAO, the Food and Agriculture Organization. There they saw a parade of international policy makers and critics who put the students' mission in a secular context, including Vandana Shiva, the Indian physicist and activist, who gave them a short, scorching lesson in the idiocies of global trade policies and preventable starvation. In turn, two of the graduating students got to stand up and address the internationally known speakers. Saccá managed the conference, shuffling name cards at the big table onstage in the UN building near the Hippodrome, as the world activists, Harvard professors, journalists, and policy experts came and went through the day.

During the lectures, I sat next to the anthropology professor who trains the students in the uses of geographic information systems. "It's the ultimate interdisciplinary tool," Barrett Brenton enthused, and the parade of speakers with their charts and maps illustrating the feminization of poverty and the proliferation of AIDS orphans was punctuated by Brenton leaning over to whisper, "GIS—see that chart? GIS made that possible."

The new St. John's group benefited by being the third class to run the technological gauntlet with the librarians. Shaughnessy and Rioux had spent a week with the first class and two weeks with the next, and keeping them all online and wired through the year had been exhausting. Even two weeks, the librarians learned, was not quite long enough to overcome the students' cultural shyness, second-language issues, and technostress, and when they left for home, Shaughnessy said, "I felt like I was abandoning them." A few of the far-flung students never really got the hang of Refworks, the program that allowed them to save and organize all their online sources, turning their desire to fight hunger, disease, and discrimination into scholarly papers; instead they laboriously typed up footnotes and citations, an old-fashioned waste of time. That, Shaughnessy felt, constituted a failure on her part, and "in a few cases, you didn't know whether they just couldn't use Refworks or they didn't have connectivity." So she and Rioux were staying in Rome with this latest class for the entire month of their initiation. There were opportunities for one-on-one sessions, and classes like this, a whole session devoted to this bibliographic organizing tool.

I sat between two young students, one from Kenya and one from Nigeria. Cara from San Diego and Jean from New Jersey mingled with priests from India and Ghana, four students from the Philippines, and a Cambodian. The Nigerian, Sister Bibiana, wore a simple cropped veil. "Now we're going to open an Internet window," Shaughnessy said, and her Think-Pad screen projected that page to the whole class. "When we opened our accounts last time, we got an error, remember?" Rioux jumped in, cheerleading: "And who's afraid? None of

us!" Shaughnessy entered the password, and an error message
came up. "Remember I mentioned Saint Jerome, the patron
saint of libraries? Add Jerome as a 'trusted site' during login,
then you're okay to enter."

It took twenty minutes to get everyone through the password and into the Refworks database. While Rioux worked
on someone's stubborn laptop, Shaughnessy guided the class
through a search for information about rehabilitation in prison
populations, Sister Bibiana's special interest. Her search called
up 7,699 resources. "I think you got some information here,
Sister." Shaughnessy showed the class how to refine and narrow
the search by subject; then she whittled it down to just scholarly
journals—and thousands of articles turned into seventeen.

What seemed like a miracle from a distance was simply the
librarian showing them how to find and save important information and organize it in a useful way. But nothing looked
so magical as when she clicked to show all those sources lined
up like rows of wheat or beans, in perfect Modern Language
Association style: author's name, then title, then publication,
then all the other details; and then she clicked again, and instantly the format changed. Now the same sources appeared in
American Psychological Association style, with the author's
name, then the date. The class gasped. Rioux told them: "This
is the style you'll use if you're doing a scientific paper, because
the date appears right after the author's name. The date matters
more to scientists."

There was joy in the missionaries' classroom. "Wow, wow!"
the students said, sending their folders full of the heartaches and

miseries of the world zipping through cyberspace. Shaughnessy grinned at me. "Isn't it great when people get as excited as we do about information resources?"

"You all will use and reuse the UN Declaration of Human Rights, so put that in your folder now," Rioux counseled them. "And look, if you lose something, it wouldn't be tragic, because you can always generate it again."

"Hopefully, this makes you a little less anxious," Shaughnessy said, and obviously it had; the students who streamed out of the classroom looked like the wrinkles had been ironed out of their foreheads, and Sister Bibiana was beaming. Afterward, Shaughnessy commiserated over their challenges: "I cannot even imagine how hard it is for them." Rioux called out after the students, "I sent you all a *BusinessWeek* article about information services and restrictions on cybercafés in India. Read if you want, and we'll chat at dinner."

The librarians' organizing for the greater good had already had an impact. After class, Shaughnessy made me a copy of a homemade facebook one of the new American students had compiled on his own initiative. In addition to photos of each new student and each administrator, with addresses, e-mails, and birthdays, he had drawn up a list broken down by time zones. When it was noon in the Philippines and seven a.m. in Kenya, it was nine p.m. in San Diego and midnight at St. John's in Queens.

Another of Shaughnessy and Rioux's students, a former detective from Brooklyn, has already announced what she wants to do when she finishes this program and her thesis on the use of information systems in the Congo. She will soon begin studies for a St. John's master's in Library and Information Science, and follow in Shaughnessy and Rioux's footsteps. "Being a researcher is no different than being a detective," Evelyn Cruz told me.

A friendly, burly man in shorts and sneakers, Kevin Rioux wrote his master's thesis on inhalant abuse on the Mexican border; he managed to discuss the horrors of the world without delusion while maintaining a cheerful, upbeat face. "I grew up in New Orleans, but I was born in Maine. I'm French-Canadian, not Cajun." His mother was on the last plane out of New Orleans before Katrina hit, and found herself in Houston, among people who had no sympathy for those who didn't evacuate. "Some people have no idea what it's like to live without a credit card," Rioux said, shaking his head. He was passionate about social justice, and had written a number of scholarly papers that link everyday library and information practice with human rights goals. He mentioned Shaughnessy's education in philosophy, and said, "We're trying to find a philosophical framework for this work. The Vincentians are conservative, but they're humane, and that's important to us; and we have our intellectual freedom." The *we* is personal: Kathy Shaughnessy and Kevin Rioux planned to marry between the time the first class graduated in late July and the beginning of the first semester in late August—not in Rome, which would have been lovely, but in Shaughnessy's hometown, Baltimore; her family is too large to travel, and marrying without their presence was unthinkable. "I know, Baltimore in August,"

Shaughnessy said with a laugh. Her mother suggested several alternative dates, but, "No, it pretty much has to be the sixteenth," she told her.

So, between the impending graduation and the marriage of the professors their students called "the special K's," jubilation was what I expected to find the next day. Instead I discovered Shaughnessy sitting at a table in the open lounge, stricken. While the librarians and other faculty members had been toiling in Rome, and university administrators were on their way to Italy to celebrate the first graduating class in this program, the library on the St. John's home campus in Queens was losing some of its space. Now workmen on the upper floors had damaged pipes, flooding the librarians' offices and soaking some of the stacks and the computer lab and archives downstairs. While she'd been teaching students how to stay wired and connected in a disaster-fraught world, an apparently preventable disaster had devastated the library back home.

"It will take us years to recover," Rioux said later, with typical pragmatic directness. "We've been told we'll have to work from home next semester. You can't have a university of fifteen thousand students without a library. If we didn't have our online resources, we'd have to shut the university." The anthropology professor was keeping them posted; his wife, the university's archivist, was picking through the damaged collections and e-mailing details of the bad news.

The faculty members worked hard to master their emotions in front of the students. They refused to let the wreckage of their stateside library dim the celebration. The carafe of red wine on the dining table usually sat untouched, but on the last day of classes, wine found its way into the students' glasses, as a feeling of giddiness began to filter into the halls.

There were so many priests at the altar of St. Peter's Pontifical Oratorio Chapel, I felt like I was in a seminary. Everyone wanted to take part in this graduation. In the airy, modern chapel tucked in a fragrant hillside a few miles from the Idente residence, an impressive procession of priests, monsignors, and even a cardinal coming down the aisle opened the ceremonies. They would celebrate Mass, and then we'd all move to the plusher auditorium for the graduation ceremony, first in English, then Italian. The only priest I recognized was Father Jean-Pierre Ruiz, the director of the Social Justice program; during lunch he had kindly and articulately explained some of the Church's policies to me.

Unlike the splendid baroque churches I had visited in Rome, this one was modern polished brick, with a stark crucifix on the altar and a modern metal sculpture running along the walls to indicate the Stations of the Cross—it looked like barbed wire. The interior was no competition for the glory of the suits and saris and academic robes of the graduates and their people. Here they were, *in Rome,* in a place and time they had struggled to get to, and they were beaming. Parnel's baby, fussing, was gathered up by one of the new students, who took him to the vestibule and rocked him. In an alcove near the altar, a group from the Philippines sang the Alleluia joyously and energetically. They ended with multiple harmonies that echoed through the chapel.

I had sat through a long childhood of Masses, and long ago swore I'd never sit through another, but there I was, believing, if not in the risen Savior, then *something*. I murmured bits of the old familiar prayers. Jeff Olson sat respectfully, head bowed, while the others knelt or walked up to take Communion; but when one of the priests announced it was time to wish each other peace, I grasped Olson's hand, and Shaughnessy's, and Rioux's, and sought out Saccá's and the woman who was responsible for the program's summer home in the Idente residence. "Peace, sister; peace, brother." I waved to the students across the aisle and they waved back. It was impossible for me not to feel an emotional stake in their struggles and their future peace.

The frocked men in the front of the chapel had decided beforehand who would give the benediction, who would pass out Communion, and who would deliver the sermon; they had split up the duties, so all could participate. The sermon was assigned to a priest who wasn't part of the Social Justice group and perhaps didn't quite understand how it worked. "Our obsession with and dependence on technology is frightening," he intoned. "BlackBerries, cell phones, the Internet, navigation systems, and remote controls—we are addicted to them. How many hours slip by? Do they make our lives easier? Simpler? Have they freed us for more quality moments, or simply made us busier?" I looked sideways as Shaughnessy sighed beside me. The students listened with deference. Olson's face betrayed nothing. The librarians had constructed a cyber-network full of those very things that missionaries and human rights workers were using to further their work. Against all odds, and in spite of typhoons, figurative and real, they would stop long enough to celebrate a graduation and a marriage. But they had some work to do with their own people. They had to explain to at least one old-fashioned priest that it was all that technology that made this particular mission possible.

7.

TO THE RAMPARTS!

"There's a subversive element to librarianship that I adore."

_____

The most visible change to librarianship in the past generation is maybe the simplest: librarians have left the building.
Waiting behind the reference desk for patrons to approach is
old-fashioned. Passive is passé. If people who needed library
services are in the streets, that's where some librarians vowed
to be—at any rate, that was the impetus behind Radical
Reference. Librarians to the ramparts!

Spotted in the street at the Republican National Convention in Minneapolis/St. Paul in 2008 were several young
women carrying signs that read "Street Librarian." Members
of the Minneapolis chapter of Radical Reference, they were
armed with iPhones bookmarked to a wiki loaded with information about political candidates and schedules, the Twin
Cities, public toilets, fast food, and legal aid. And they were
linked on Twitter. "Twitter really saved us a couple of times

from dangerous situations," librarian Wanda Marsolek wrote me. Twitter alerted them to street closings, as well as "where the police were arresting people, and where the police were using force. . . . Despite the fear of being arrested, tear gassed, having concussion grenades thrown at us and being trampled by horses, I am really glad I was there, to see it firsthand and provide information for those out in the streets." Her colleague, Lacey Prpic Hedtke, said the decision to take such risks wasn't difficult. "I'm a librarian . . . why *shouldn't* I do something?" They *could* help, so they would.

Radical Reference, the organization that inspired them, was born in the days before the previous Republican convention, when Jenna Freedman, who earned notice in 2003 as one of *Library Journal*'s Movers and Shakers—young librarians already having an impact on the profession—came up with the idea to provide reference support to the demonstrators. "I was sitting in a No Republican National Convention Clearinghouse meeting and feeling out of it," said Freedman. "There I was in my thirties, in this room full of twenty-something crusty punks and people who already had their affinity groups—and especially in an activist community, you can't just say, 'Hey, I want to help.' They'll think you're a cop, or just weird. So, I thought, 'What can I do as a librarian?'"

Freedman has blue hair, or usually she has blue hair, when she gets around to coloring it. She doesn't do fashion otherwise— "I'm not a panty-hose librarian"—though a feathery boa-like scarf lent a jaunty touch to her black pants and shirt the day I visited her at the Barnard College Library, where she has the eminently respectable job of coordinator of reference services. She's an academic librarian who has been called an anarchist librarian, not in the sense of bombing the stacks or even causing mischief there—in the sense of sharing information freely, serving people instead of rules (or rulers), and continually questioning authority. Alternate sources of information and culture were her passion. Freedman shared an office, so she found a quiet room where we could talk privately: a supply closet. The librarian who helped propel her colleagues to the streets climbed into the closet behind me and together we relived the largest protest at a convention in U.S. history.

"People were not excited about the Republicans having their convention in New York City and exploiting the memory of 9/11. There was a lot of anger in libraryland. I had the idea of supporting the demonstration, but I won't take credit for inventing or coming up with Radical Reference. There were five or six of us at first. As soon as we started putting the word out, people were really excited and rushed in to help."

It was clear from the beginning that New York City would be hosting, along with the Republicans, hundreds of thousands of antiwar demonstrators, AIDS activists, militant bicyclists, abortion activists (prochoice and antiabortion), and others. The atmosphere was not expected to be friendly; police would be out in force, not to protect the protesters and their right to free expression, but to arrest them. And since rumors are the engines of mobs, these protesters would need information they could trust.

Eric Goldhagen, an open-source software designer who

later married Freedman, and his colleagues at the Inter-Activist Network helped the core group fashion a website, RadicalReference.info, with the banner "Answers for Those Who Question Authority." It was classy enough to have its own logo, a lowercase *i* (the international symbol for information) against a background of six orange bars, the *I Ching* symbol for "Strong action will be supremely blessed. Keep on." Activists and independent journalists were encouraged to post questions that this pool of librarians would answer. The librarians' enticements were wonderfully librarian-like: "We've got access to hundreds of expensive subscription databases, and we know how to use them." From the start, Radical Reference tried to serve activists across the spectrum; the website stated unequivocally that "we provide services regardless of political leaning." The librarians compiled reference links for the site, with information about alternative libraries, bicycling resources, voting, and the USA Patriot Act, and had the site ready to launch by convention time. After helping fact-check *The People's Guide to the Republican National Convention* and running a workshop on fact-checking for independent journalists, the Radical Reference librarians suited up and joined the waves of protesters who swarmed New York late that summer.

"Librarians by nature are not really confrontational people," Freedman said. "It's kind of weird to stand in the street with our little cap or T-shirt, handing things out. And we carried Ready Reference Kits, which were binders that had information like the day's events and the schedule. We had a map that showed where the bathrooms were. We had the phone

number for central booking. We had a little handout on the
Patriot Act. . . ."

They had numbers for emergency legal services, details on
area restaurants, copies of laws governing assembly and protest.
So they could alert one another to trouble spots and police
cordons, they used a mass text-messaging service designed especially for activists, called TXTmob, which inspired Twitter.
And they had backup: on-call librarians with computers and
access to reliable databases and reference materials. They
circulated among and served not just the 500,000 people
marching in the United for Peace and Justice protest, but
the thousands of other protesters in multiple other actions.
(The famous protest at the 1968 Democratic convention in
Chicago, by contrast, drew 10,000.) Freedman detailed the
experience in her zine. The librarian wrote: "Demonstrators
at the RNC outnumbered delegates by some outrageous ratio,
and I'm not talking about the half million that were at the big
United for Peace demo. I'm talking about the thousands of
outside agitators that came into town to tell the Republicans
to fuck off. . . . I'm proud to have been a part of it."

Over the next three years, hundreds of librarians, library
students, and library clerks joined Radical Reference, and local
collectives formed in Los Angeles, Boston, New York, Tucson,
Austin, and Milwaukee. The idea of librarians serving ad hoc
populations like crowds of demonstrators has spread across
the country and beyond—there's even a RadRef chapter in
Bangalore, India.

I was hearing about all this in a badly lit supply closet,

among buckets and broken chairs and reams of copy paper, in the neighborhood where student protests had brought Barnard's brother college, Columbia, grinding to a halt in 1968. Our conversation had a conspiratorial feel, heightened by the fact that we were keeping our voices low in deference to the students and librarians on the other side of the door. "Death to ignorance!" Freedman might have been whispering. "Power to the people! Pssst! Catalog the revolution!"

Like most wired librarians, Jenna Freedman can be found all over the Web, posting whimsy on social networks and thoughtful commentary in library publications. She has a blog, *Lower East Side Librarian*, in which she writes about everything from vampire fiction to roller derby to politics. She's also active offline, publishing her zine, *Lower East Side Librarian Winter Solstice Shout-Out*, as well as organizing a feminist zine collection for the Barnard College Library. Zines, homemade, self-published periodicals, are rich artifacts of offbeat and street culture; they aren't collected by most libraries or archives, though there are exceptions, like the Salt Lake City Public Library. Jenna Freedman's vision as a librarian encompassed electronic networks of activist information professionals, as well as old-fashioned displays of low-tech, handwritten booklets.

I wanted to research her work before we met, easily done on her website and Barnard's; but trying to get my hands on her zine was more challenging, because I had to buy it directly from her. I sent her an e-mail and mentioned why I was interested. Instead of a warm greeting and instructions on how to deposit a few bucks to her PayPal account, I got a response from Freedman that showed a bit of teeth. "I'd like to hear more about your book. Any particular librarians (or kind of librarians) you're writing about? Sorry to get all reference on you, but I hesitate to send out intimate details about the last seven years of my life without much knowledge of who wants it and why." She'd found my website, and wanted verification that she had the right person.

"'Sorry to get all reference on you'?" What a great phrase. But wait a minute—she published these intimate details of her life, but only certain people could read them? Zines may be self-published, but they're *published*. Freedman had written about the difference between blogs and zines, and her response was the perfect illustration of the difference. You hit the post button on a blog, and your sentences flow into cyberspace where anyone from your kindergarten babysitter to your boss can read them. You run your zine through the copier, and fold it up, and you can pretty much track it through the world. The humble zine is revealing in a way that drunken photos on MySpace never could be. "I'm pretty intimate in my zine," she acknowledged after sending me the complete set.

There was some of Freedman's DNA on every page of *Lower East Side Librarian Winter Solstice Shout-Out*: the accomplished but self-doubting young librarian; the city dweller who hated cars and seriously feared plants (she'd been told at an impressionable age about a cancer that grew inside someone, and pictured green tendrils); the bride who'd celebrated with a vegan cake made of Rice Krispies, lactose-free Rice

Dream, and Marshmallow Fluff; the urban woman who kept a separate apartment from her beloved spouse and cats (though if they could afford a place big enough to share . . .). She read constantly in women's literature, but had skipped Jane Austen till she was almost forty. She was the daughter of a former social worker, now a Hindu nun, and the prominent librarian Maurice (Mitch) Freedman, who had been the director of the Westchester Library System and the president of the American Library Association. "If my father weren't a librarian," she told me, "I might have been one a lot sooner, which isn't a slam on my father. It's just like you want to be your own person and do your own thing. . . . I finally stopped resisting it." For all her political activism and digital-age networking, she espoused the plain and simple model of the librarian. "I like the word 'reader' for library patron," she declared in her zine, "especially compared to 'customer,' which is favored by so many public libraries doing their best to adopt a business model, thus destroying librarianship's best strength: our emphasis on service. . . ."

Like the zines she collected, hers was the chronicle of a complicated, unique, and direct voice. It was both more open and more substantial than her blog; it had been written, not dashed off, the whole package crafted. "[Z]ines, although they're called ephemera in library lingo, are actually a lot more permanent than blogs," she wrote.

Zines were ephemera? I remember the first time I heard the word *ephemera* used in connection with libraries. I was in Edinburgh, hanging out at the Fringe Festival, a cacophonous arts event with hundreds of shows and performances conducted on the street and in makeshift venues, alive with the raw, fun power of undiscovered actors mugging and posing. I had just started tracking librarians, so between a comedy act put on by a guy who had sailed the English Channel in a bathtub and a performance of *A Midsummer Night's Dream* featuring a Puck with an artificial member bobbing from his belt, I ducked into the National Library of Scotland and browsed their special collections. There I met a friendly librarian with the haunting name of Eoin Shalloo.

Shalloo tried to explain his library's more mysterious holdings, the Fleming of Wigtown Papers and something called *The Roit or Quheill of Tyme.* The Flemings were earls of Wigtown, landowners and fancy types, fond of keeping old receipts, all the way back to the fifteenth century. *The Roit or Quheill of Tyme* was an anonymous chronicle of kings from the beginning of time to 1537. Among other old papers, Shalloo was also guarding the minutes of meetings about the running of a soup kitchen from the mid-nineteenth century—great background for scholars of soup kitchens, no? What about the Fringe Festival? I asked. Wasn't that an important Scottish event happening right under your window? He allowed that the festival was of historic interest, and that certain records pertaining to it would merit collecting, if someone were to bother to collect them. I had in my bag a cluster of flyers the buskers and shills had pressed on me, homemade advertisements, handbills for plays, coupons for comedy shows. "Oh, we wouldn't collect those," Shalloo told me. Those were *ephemera*. So I met that lowly library word.

True, you can't collect everything, but I couldn't help pitying future students and scholars trying to re-create the Fringe Festival in Edinburgh without the litter of flyers, the trail of paper that led the audience to the performers. That would be a parade without the confetti. I still wonder why the receipts of an old soup kitchen are worth preserving in a national library, and the flyer announcing a comic Shakespeare performance with particularly creative props was considered trash.

Ephemera, that beautiful word, like *fairy dust* or *wood smoke*, is, in library science, what you toss in a box without cataloging, or throw away altogether—unless, of course, you find your niche as a collector of ephemera, like the British printer who lived on the premises of the Oxford University Press with the job of keeping it running during World War II; his only amusement during the period in which he threw his body between the bombs and the press was to collect advertising circulars, handbills promoting entertainment, and notices of executions—historic ephemera. Now the John Johnson Collection of Printed Ephemera is part of the Bodleian Library at Oxford, a rare source, so claims the Bodleian, of primary historic documents. No fewer than 65,000 of these once-disposable scraps of paper have been deemed important enough to be digitally preserved, and can be found on ProQuest, a database you can probably access online with your library card.

All of which is to say: one person's trash is another's history.

Eoin Shalloo's ephemera was John Johnson's history and Jenna Freedman's archive of zines.

I must be an ephemerist; as soon as someone tells me something is not worth saving, I want to argue. The regular weeding that librarians do, removing dated or moldy old books, throwing out or giving away old copies, even of *Reader's Digest* condensed books, makes me nervous. The blog *Awful Library Books* is an effort by two public librarians to highlight discarded books so ridiculous and out-of-date, even a hoarder like me will agree they need to be ditched. The blog features, mockingly, *More Great Pantyhose Crafts* (1985), *Creative Recreation for the Mentally Retarded* (1975), and fifty-year-old books on gas prices, computers, space exploration, the Soviet Union, and careers for girls. It's entertaining, I admit, and I see their point; but I wish they'd link the pictures of decrepit book covers to digital copies of the books. Frankly, I want to see what's inside *Those Amazing Leeches* (1988). In fact, I'd love a ramshackle little hut of a library that carried nothing but copies of discards and awful books from the narrow tunnel of our past—books that captured us as we were. Reminders of how foolish writers sometimes look can be instructive. And these books tell our history, too.

The Barnard Zine Collection resided in the middle of the floor, between a rack of magazines and the reference desk, in an oblong wooden caddy designed to hold periodicals on all four sides. The zines had a distinctly homemade look, their poetic titles often written by hand and poking above their shelf-mates: *I Dreamed I Was Assertive*; *Ben Is Dead*; *No, I Don't Think So*; *Placenta*; *Darling Disasters*. A few of them looked like works of art, the creative vessels of zinesters like Celia Perez, also a librarian, whose mock encyclopedia *The Miscellaneous History of Common Experiments* was a collage of words, paint strips, glassine envelopes with foreign stamps, and a glossy map of Chicago. Mostly, though, the zines looked as if they had been made at someone's kitchen table.

Like any collection, this one benefited from the collector's, or librarian's, focus. This wasn't just stuff that happened to be in zine format; it had to fit with the rest of the library's holdings, in a library that served an undergraduate population of women and contained archives and manuscripts of women authors. "I feel like it's important for each library to have its niche," Freedman said, so Barnard's zine collection was restricted to zines of urban females. "I'm definitely missing out on some good wacky zine fun," she allowed. She shipped those that didn't fit in her collection to other zine libraries. Queer zines (male) went to the Queer Zine Archive Project in Milwaukee, where they were not only collected and cataloged but (with the permission of the zinesters) scanned into a searchable Web archive; transgender zines went to Kelly Shortandqueer at the Denver Zine Library.

Zines represent a challenge to a cataloger with their nonpaper extras (buttons, tea bags, locks of hair), their nonstandard sizes, covers that left no room for cataloging information, and often mysterious origins. "There is no preexisting librarians' code pertaining to how one should handle a document that

TO THE RAMPARTS! 117

includes a free prophylactic," a reporter for the *Boston Globe* wrote. Zines are hard to categorize. The librarian who tried to organize them geographically would be frustrated; zine-sters tend to be peripatetic, or disappear altogether. Freedman and her colleagues tried to fit the individual zines into the Library of Congress Classification System, but the zines were too miscellaneous. They ended up classified simply as zines and alphabetized by author. Freedman's goal was to make the zines an integral part of the Barnard and Columbia catalog, and findable both inside and outside the community; listings on WorldCat had led to interlibrary loans and a higher profile. She wanted them to be accessible and circulate to the student population, but she also wanted them preserved in the archives, for current and future scholars. One of her mentors gave her the idea of collecting two copies. "First copy goes in the acid free climate controlled archive, and the second copy, if there is one, goes into the stacks which can now be circulated. It allows me to be much less precious about the stack zines because I know that the zines in the archive are okay."

She handed me a mini-zine, an 11- by 17-inch folded paper called *Cite This Zine! How to Cite a Zine in Your Research Project*, conceived and created by an intern. The zine lays a path for this material to be included in scholarly papers; now maybe zines will get footnoted in the ongoing history of our culture. Freedman herself has written technical articles about cataloging and collecting zines for librarians—she sees them as important primary sources of underdocumented subcultures. "We preserve today what may be important later," she said.

The Barnard College Library website had pages dedicated to the zine collection that made the case for this collection of more than seventeen hundred voices, beginning with an excerpt from Jenny San Diego's zine *Not Sorry*: "I'm not even trying to be dramatic, but to the world at large, I am a freak . . . a fat, queer, mentally ill, politically radical woman with very little money and little to no regard for beauty standards and so on and so forth. But you know what? I am so NOT fucking SORRY . . . my experiences, ideas and opinions need to be heard. . . . Besides, how else are these stories going to be documented? . . . Now I know that this zine will not go much beyond the zine reading community, but this is where I have chosen to start and it's something which is always better than nothing."

I curled up with a couple of librarian zines, including *Riot Librarrrian* (after the "riot grrrl" feminist punk movement). The whole concept of a librarian zinester intrigued me, implying as it did a person who could zip around databases, link to the world of information, and still want to sit down in her free time to cut-and-paste a homemade expressive booklet. (I wasn't the only one intrigued; a library student at the University of Wisconsin, Madison, had started the Library Workers Zine Collection, to preserve alternative voices in the field.) "One of the reasons I decided to enter this profession," one of the *Riot Librarrrians* wrote, "was because I'm in love with information, and the library remains one of the few spaces in our lives where information is not a commodity. . . . There's a subversive element to librarianship that I adore."

That's the ticket: "one of the few spaces in our lives where information is not a commodity." It's no wonder I kept running into librarians who struck simple notes in a complicated world. Riot Librarrrian's e-mail address was printed on the inside cover along with the request, "Please do not stalk." Would I be stalking if I sent the writers an e-mail? I decided to risk it. Zines were the call in a call-and-response; "I never got so many letters until I made a zine," Freedman said. Not surprisingly, though, my e-mail came bouncing back. I pictured the two itinerant librarians, their backpacks filled with laptops or smart phones, definitely paper, library paste, scissors—and a bunch of extra *r*'s.

I went on a zine kick after meeting Freedman, another diversion into the low-tech stacks behind the library computers. (But even straight-up digital librarians will tell you that that's half the fun of this business, getting diverted.) I attended a panel on the subject, got myself on some mailing lists, and came across a zine that recounted the story of an unusual life.

Zines are most valuable, it seems to me, as documentary artifacts and narratives when written by people who are hard to categorize: strays, self-identified women, men, transgenders, agitators, street people, punks, anyone who didn't fit neatly in a society that organizes itself in simple binary categories—male or female, Democrat or Republican, black or white, married or single, adult or child. The author of the unusual zine I read had been an unhappy girl, until *she* started calling herself *he* and began a course of male hormones. After growing a beard and deepening his voice, but stopping short of surgery, he embarked on a relationship with a transvestite male. The self-defined male with female parts lived with a male who preferred to dress as a female. What were they? A couple. What was *he*? Even he wasn't sure, though *he* felt right. The zine was a record of his unique life, which he felt a responsibility to document.

Who knows how many people are invisible because their stories don't fit our categories?

Librarians have long tried to catalog the world in all its complexity. They want to describe things accurately, find the right name for this bird or that; but they are also looking for a description that fits into the architecture of information, that shows where the bird fits in its family, genus, species, and so on. They argue passionately about the specifics. Freedman and her father both referred me to the work of Sanford (Sandy) Berman, a radical librarian from Minnesota who wrote, among others, a book called *The Joy of Cataloging*. Berman has spent decades combing the Library of Congress's subject headings, petitioning its catalogers for refinements, deletions, and additions to overlooked or culturally insensitive topics—arguing that they need to distinguish between the god of Christianity and other gods, that Armenian massacre should be Armenian genocide, that Prostitutes cry out to gather with Exotic dancers and Erotic film actors under the umbrella Sex workers.

Library catalogers try to describe things neutrally and avoid cultural bias. They also try to sidestep the holes that open up and swallow our questions when we can't find what we're looking for—what Berman calls "bibliocide by cataloging." Subject headings, search terms, keywords—if the searcher can't figure out the right term, the one that triggers the jackpot of information, she's lost. In her memoir *One Drop: My Father's Hidden Life—A Story of Race and Family Secrets,* Bliss Broyard described going to the Boston Public Library to look for stories about people like her father, the critic Anatole Broyard, who had been born Creole but passed for white. *Passing*—that's the term she looked for in the card catalog, but she found only Passing (Football), Miscegenation, and Mulatto, none of which led to stories of people who had been born one race and lived another. As far as she could tell, the world of the early 1990s was devoid of books about racial passing. Broyard thought she was an outsider, unconnected to anything in the vast world of written literature. Now there's a subject heading in the Library of Congress called Passing (Identity) that marks a path to Bliss Broyard's book, among all the others.

But the catalog is incomplete on the subject of librarians. There are Library of Congress subject headings for Bisexual librarians, Gay librarians, Transgender librarians, Transsexual librarians, and Packhorse librarians, the last of these, librarians "who delivered books on horseback to patrons in the remote rural areas in the United States in the 1930s." But Anarchist librarians? You can't find them in the catalog. Not yet, anyway.

8.

FOLLOW THAT TATTOOED LIBRARIAN

As a rule, librarians cultivate a professionalism that projects
sexual neutrality, which permits them to guard their trove
of both innocent and risqué books from a position of high-
minded principle, and also helps keep the stalkers at bay.

Jenna Freedman is one of *Library Journal*'s "Movers and Shakers," and she is also one of the Library Society of the World's self-nominated "Shovers and Makers" ("S & M," for short). "Jenna Freedman has always been a late bloomer," she begins, then ends her mock citation by listing, among her other notable accomplishments, "worshipping my cats." Along with their serious, academic, and specialized affiliations, many of the librarians I followed belonged to satiric groups like this one, "the greatest dis-organization of librarians and library fans ever!" The Library Society of the World offered T-shirts for sale, emblazoned with their mascot, a fish. Why a fish? A typo had turned their "code of ethics" into a "cod of ethics," and they ran with it.

If you had to divide the world into creeps and assholes, as writer Susin Shapiro once did, librarians would be creeps. By and large, they're cat people, not dog people. Librarians' favorite wall decorations are posters of the goofy "LOLcats," adorable cat pictures with misspelled legends: *I Can Has Cheezburger?* or *drunk dial kitteh callin u at 2 am.* Is it the misspellings that crack them up?

As a breed, librarians tend to share a sense of humor that is quirky, sardonic, and full of wordplay, but nothing captures their gift for self-mockery quite as vividly as the book-cart drills, held at various state conferences and culminating each year in a contest at the American Library Association's summer convention. These precision-drill routines, set to music, are performed as a treat for their fellow librarians; rarely are they seen in public. I snuck in, though, and witnessed drills so elaborate and goofy I felt I'd fallen through Middle Earth into a world of elves and hobbits, or entered Willy Wonka's factory just as the Oompa-Loompas burst into song.

The competition in 2007 was held in a hangar in the Washington Convention Center, a cavernous space where a small aircraft show could comfortably fit. Librarians packed the viewing area behind the ropes, craning their necks and flashing cell phones. They hooted in appreciation as a team from Delaware filed out to open the competition, a dozen librarians in black pants and shirts, sporting bling that included rhinestone necklaces and glittering tiaras. The performers spun bookcarts suggestively and waved their various-sized fannies to a medley of "Diamonds Are a Girl's Best Friend" and "Material Girl," and took turns hanging on the arms of a large, unhealthy-looking guy in a top hat and tails, the token male librarian. For their grand finale, they lined up the book carts and the sugar daddy helped one of the women leap up and strut the length of the book-cart line right up to the judges' table. The crowd whooped and cheered. It was wildly entertaining, a sparkle of Vegas in downtown D.C.

What could possibly beat this? How about eight librarians from Ohio in black pants and bright yellow-and-black shirts, with what looked like antennae bobbing on their heads, spinning their striped yellow-and-black carts to the frantic tune of Rimsky-Korsakov's "Flight of the Bumblebee"? Now *that* was inspired; the soundtrack perfectly captured the madness of the information age. The finale featured a librarian spinning a book cart on one wheel, a feat comparable to nailing the first triple axel in the Olympics. This elicited a roar of approval from the spectators. The bee librarians zoomed away, and a different kind of glitz rolled onstage.

The Austin team wore Rosie the Riveter outfits, pedal pushers and darling embroidered denim shirts, with knotted bandannas on the tops of their heads, and moved like the June Taylor Dancers. Their choreography, to Bette Midler's rendition of "Boogie Woogie Bugle Boy," looked practically professional: a dozen attractive, foot-tapping, finger-snapping librarians, sending a dozen book carts marked "READING IS RIVETING" whizzing across the floor in coordinated waves.

It was as unfair as a contest between Miss Texas and Miss Delaware. Austin was declared the winner to raucous applause. And what did the winning team get for defeating the vamps of Delaware and the frantic buzzing bees of Ohio, after choreographing and drilling for weeks, decorating props, investing in costumes, risking ridicule? The prize was . . . a book cart.

If *you* don't mention the stereotype, librarians will, with the sly humor that seems to be the best defense against their profession's humorless image. I've got a librarian action figure on my desk, modeled on the charming real librarian Nancy Pearl, who thought up the idea of a whole town reading the same book and who wrote the bestseller *Book Lust*. When you press her back, she lifts her finger to her mouth, the old-fashioned signal authority figures use to say "*Shut up!*" The tiny shushing Nancy makes a nice tableau with my Virginia Woolf finger puppet and other bookstore novelty items.

The sexy-librarian image bothers librarians as much as the shushing business. As a rule, librarians cultivate a professionalism that projects sexual neutrality, which permits them to guard their trove of both innocent and risqué books from a position of high-minded principle, and also helps keep the stalkers at bay. But there is a tension between the businesslike and generally modest librarians and the occasionally racy books they guard that finds expression in the culture in a stream of winks and leers. Even Marion the Librarian got it. ("She advocates dirty books . . . Chaucer . . . Rabelais. . . Balzzz . . zac!")

From the description on Amazon of one of the many, many steamy books featuring librarians:

Though not quite a classic on a par with *The Librarian Loves to Lick,* and lacking the studied innocence of *Horny Peeping Librarian*, still, *The Librarian's Naughty Habit* is easily the finest account of sex and the circulation desk that we at the Olympia Press can legally do.

Enough already, some librarians grumble, but the young librarians run with it. How better to deal with the sexy-librarian trope than take it as flattery?

"I'm more like *Party Girl*," Tazmira (not her real name) told me over biryani and chicken tikka. She was referring to the 1995 indy movie in which "librarian" was the punch line of the joke: What would become of the creative, flaky party girl played by Parker Posey? As it turned out, she found her future embracing the Dewey Decimal System.

Tazmira is a beauty, with masses of dark hair shot through with exuberant streaks of pink and candy red: part Indian, part Arab. She talks fast, about the Weezer concert she is about to go to, a film festival she has just come from, her husband and grad school sweetheart—she is a children's librarian and he's a librarian for "big kids," which is to say, adults.

Tazmira and I had been Facebook friends since I discovered The Tattooed Librarian, one of her many groups. I sat around some days and amused myself by combing the lists of librarian-related organizations on the site. So far, I had found The Tattooed Librarian; No, I Don't Look Like a Librarian!; Yes, I Do Look Like a Librarian; Do I Look Like a Librarian?; Librarians Wearing Kilts; and Archivists Without Crippling Personality Disorders. And, speaking of Facebook, you know those silly quizzes, "Which Beatles song are you?" or "Which TV mom are you?" Librarians play one called "What metadata standard are you?"

Although there were dozens of photos of Tazmira in various hair styles and bright colors on her profile, her tattoos were not visible, and unlike the other tattooed librarians, she posted no pictures of them. She was careful that way—it was her child-patrons she was thinking about. She was so concerned about setting a good example for them that she didn't want me to use her real name or location.

Tazmira had traveled to Las Vegas recently to visit an old colleague and friend. She did a search beforehand (of course; what librarian *wouldn't* do a complete search before she went anywhere) to see what Vegas had to offer, and was amused to find a club called The Library. "Got to go there, don't I?" "But that's a gentleman's club!" her friend said. Tazmira laughed, undeterred. "Wouldn't it be funny to get a T-shirt? I just want a T-shirt and a beer stein that says 'The Library.' Souvenirs!"

So they went, Tazmira and her friend, and identified themselves as librarians. The man at the door invited them inside to see what he could rustle up in the way of merchandise stamped "The Library." The club was almost full, all men save for one date—and of course, the performing faux-librarians, in glasses, their hair done up in buns, dancing on poles. Tazmira ran into a couple of them in the ladies' room. They gathered around like she was some rare creature. "You're a librarian?" they said. "Yeah, yeah, tell us about your work. We want to make our act more realistic!"

The manager never found any souvenirs; had there been any to start with? However, one of his strippers had quit, and— "You wouldn't be interested in dancing, would you?" he asked Tazmira on her way out the door.

That's right, the children's librarian was offered a job as an exotic dancer in Vegas. Tazmira laughed. She had a very nice job, already, thank you.

The phenomenon of smart, funny, cool librarians was exotic enough to make front-page news in the *New York Times*, though, perhaps inevitably, the article was blighted by its headline: A HIPPER CROWD OF SHUSHERS. It seemed that a nest of adorable young librarians in Brooklyn regularly mixed information science with cocktails while toying with the stereotypes of their profession. (There were similar nests in other spots; Philadelphia was home to a group that called itself Authority Control, named for a cataloging term.) Librarians of both sexes, including "a reference librarian at a law firm, who had a tattoo of the logo from the Federal Depository Library Program peeking out of his black T-shirt sleeve," were throwing retro parties with literary themes, raising money and collecting books for literacy campaigns, and making fashion statements with eyeglasses—pink, red, green, chunky black, even cat's-eyes with rhinestones. This group, the subject of the story, called itself Desk Set, after the least-famous Katharine Hepburn–Spencer Tracy collaboration.

In that 1957 film, Hepburn played the head reference librarian in a corporate library, administering a female staff of fast-talking know-it-alls. (The script was by the first generation of Ephron wits, Phoebe and Henry.) Spencer Tracy, as the fifties version of an IT geek, installed a giant computer designed to replace the librarians. Instead, the computer overheated and crashed, and Tracy fell for Hepburn's brainy charm. The librarian saved her job and snagged her man—and, by the way, as the film made clear, librarians were absolutely still necessary in the computer age.

Desk Set, the librarian group, began as a social club. Library science students going through graduate school at different rates were losing touch with each other, so they started arranging monthly meetings in bars. Soon, they had a name, a Facebook page with more than six hundred friends, and a more ambitious agenda. They toured each other's libraries; hosted "Dance Dance Revolution" video game parties; organized book drives for Katrina victims, where the party hosts swapped cocktail chits for used paperbacks; called for "swarms" of librarians to volunteer; and threw a grand dress-up holiday affair they called *Be Still My Frosty Heart: A Biblioball*. Like every party Desk Set sponsored, the ball was sold out and the space packed with young, laughing librarians, male and female, and music loud enough to shatter the old stereotype.

• • •

The song "Librarian" by the New Zealand duo Haunted Love debuted in 2006 with a video featuring two attractive performers suited up as mock librarians, hair pulled back, glasses in place, fingers and feet tapping in disapproval as a patron committed various crimes, like scattering books through the library and sticking gum under a table. The "librarians" lure the culprit into the closed reserves with the promise of new magazines, then crush him between the movable stacks. The video recycled the usual clichés, but at least it was stylishly done.

Perhaps inevitably, a team worked up a book cart drill to the song "Librarian" at the ALA's 2008 conference in Anaheim. While recorded female voices chanted, "I want to be a librarian / I want to check out your books. / Please give them to me / With the bar code . . . facing . . . up!" the real librarians, with open books somehow secured to their heads, spun their carts and mouthed the lyrics with relish. In unison, they scooped their hands in front of their breasts: "I want . . . to check out . . . your books."

The librarians in the audience roared.

9.

WIZARDS OF ODD

Marilena and Hypatia hovered above the virtual
library like Tinker Bells. . . . "Will you look at that,"
Cathy marveled and called another librarian over.
Together, they gaped at my screen. "That's a librarian?"

Late spring, the twenty-first century, the wired house. One
teenager video-chatting, the other on Xbox LIVE shooting
cartoon soldiers manipulated by people from around the
world, though mainly from his school. They both talk to their
screens. I'm in the kitchen playing word games on Facebook;
in the background, an old-fashioned baseball game plays out
on television. *Ding!* comes an e-mail, a message from the
virtual-reality site Second Life: spontaneous party at the Jazz
Cat. "Put on your dance clothes and come shake it."

It's not a real party in the sense that I have to drive anywhere
or be seen by others. I can't remember the last time I went to
a spontaneous party in real life. On Second Life it happens all

the time. This one was organized by Hollyjean for a network
of Second Life librarians and library lovers who call themselves
InfoGroupies; they help provide reference services for avatars.
Avatars—the forms we take to represent ourselves onscreen.

> We love information. Reading, writing, and research-
> ing information makes us happy. We love talking about
> information. Sometimes we even have useful informa-
> tion! But mostly we use our vast stores of information to
> amuse ourselves and others.

Without moving from my kitchen perch, I click on the
pale-green hand that launches the Second Life application. My
screen fills with a cliffside vista, the view from the castle I rent
for a few (real) dollars a month. The leggy animated figure
inside is my avatar, Marilena Basevi. Using the computer's
space bar and built-in mouse, I move her around corners and
up the stairs to her dressing room. In a modern version of paper
dolls, I dress her. I click open my inventory of outfits, some of
which I charged to my (real) credit card, a few pennies here,
a few bucks there. The invitation said it was a casual party,
and in person I'm casual, but in Second Life, my alter ego is a
clotheshorse with a collection of more than a hundred outfits.
I drag one of my favorites, *golddigger cocktail dress (hard steel)*,
onto Marilena's form and, presto, her old outfit disappears and
her new one materializes.

Then I find the address of the Jazz Cat Club in my landmarks file and click it so as to teleport—just like in *Star Trek*—to the party. The screen goes black with an audible whoosh, then resolves on the outskirts of a swanky open-air nightclub suspended over a shimmering lake and encircled by trees strung with tiny white lights. The dance floor is full of swaying avatars. Our hostess, the dishy blond Hollyjean, grooves and dances on top of a black piano.

A gentleman avatar named Waldron offers to dance with Marilena, via an instant message in the chat window, so we each click on a ball on the dance floor marked *waltz* (the one who leads clicks the blue ball, which triggers a dance script; the other clicks the pink one to follow). This causes the avatars to leap together and dip and sway in sync. I click a quarter-note at the bottom of the screen and the music of Frank Sinatra is piped into my kitchen, compliments of Martini in the Morning, which streams rat pack music on the Internet.

Marilena is acting out this pantomime on a set designed by a librarian from North Carolina. Someone from the cornfields of Illinois is running the avatar Hollyjean; Waldron is the stand-in for a university librarian in Toronto. It feels like round midnight in the Jazz Cat, but each of us is in real time, too—for the Brits and Germans it's the wee, wee hours; it's evening on the East Coast of the U.S. The Australians are having a jazz break midday.

In *real life*, as we all persist in calling it, I don't look like Marilena, I don't dance, and I don't listen to Frank Sinatra. But what can I do? I heard there were librarians on Second

Life, and my job is to chase librarians, even if I have to dive into the computer and go where I would never ordinarily go. I created Marilena, control her every move, and speak for her, but she has her own personality; she's the front babe I send to do reconnaissance on the 3-D web, a useful extroverted extension of me. During the slow windups and long pitching changes of a baseball game (and my life) I manipulate this little doll-like figure and act out scenes of retro-sophistication while eavesdropping on librarians, their groupies, and mates.

After more than a year of crashing librarian parties on Second Life, I can tell you where the conversation is going. The avatars will exclaim with enthusiasm over their outfits and the ambitious projects they're working on in virtual reality and grumble about their real lives; Hollyjean or Abbey Zenith or one of the other energetic librarian-avatars will cook up a new project. And I guarantee, one of the dancing librarians will bring up cataloging. Even at a sixties-themed bash Marilena crashed, full of tie-died and miniskirted librarian-avatars passing around virtual joints and gyrating to Hendrix, the Stones, and the Grateful Dead under a suspended VW bus—a party held at the librarians' other social hot spot, TX950, named for the Library of Congress call number for clubs and bars—the librarians couldn't help themselves.

"Hated cataloging . . ."

"Have you all cataloged your inventories?"

"Was Dewey a hippie?"

"I'm in the middle of a cataloging nightmare and I'm not even a cataloger. . . ."

I first learned about this world from a blog called *Librarian Avengers*. "I just spoke with a gentleman who helps run Second Life," Erica Firment wrote, "and he informed me that there are, like, a billion librarians there." These librarians apparently owned a bunch of islands and somehow had found a way to practice their profession in virtual reality. Firment, the Librarian Avenger, ended her post with a smirk: "Are we cool or what?"

I couldn't picture a website with 3-D graphics, crawling with librarians. Were the skies of Second Life thick with flying librarians in capes and glasses? I'd read a flurry of stories about someone who divorced her husband after he "married" his Second Life girlfriend; it sounded like a wild place. What were librarians doing there? Trying hard, as one early source put it, "to prove we're not sexually repressed geeks"? The term *virtual librarian* had been coined to describe librarians who provided real-time help to their patrons from a distance, using chat services on computers or phones. A whole new type of virtual librarian was being invented in Second Life, little cartoon figures who could interact visually as well—*extreme* virtual librarians. And while they were at it, these librarians were inventing another kind of library, one their patrons could walk (or fly) around in—without either librarian or patron having to leave her kitchen stool.

I installed the free Second Life software, chose a password and a stock avatar, made up my own first name and picked my surname from a list provided by the creators and maintainers of this place, Linden Lab, which launched the Second Life grid in 2003. Unlike the dozens of other virtual-reality sites, Second Life is created by its residents, so though some people complain there is nothing to *do* here, it seems to be an ideal laboratory for creative and technically savvy types who for one reason or another want to operate, like the Wizard of Oz, behind the curtain of a nickname and an avatar. As one of the librarian-avatars put it: "Linden created a laboratory and let the lab rats have the tools."

For weeks, I practiced being "in-world," learning how to walk and fly without crashing into virtual buildings, how to simultaneously move my avatar and conduct an instant-message conversation with someone else's. That required dexterity. My goal was simple: to work up the nerve and skill to visit the libraries and interview the librarians. I edited my profile so that anyone who interacted with Marilena would know there was a reporter at the controls.

One night I teleported over to the Info Island, and found an avatar with a sign floating over her head that said "Reference." Georgette was sitting on a virtual park bench. Her dark skin glowed; she wore a swirly skirt and a peach-colored sweater she told me she paid fifty Linden dollars for—about fifty U.S. cents. Every few seconds, she took a big swig from a steaming cup of coffee in her hand. "Would you like a cup?" she wrote in our instant-message box. *Ding!* A little blue box popped up on my screen: *Georgette has offered you an item from her inventory. Accept?* I accepted, and, locating the *new steam-*

ing cup of coffee in my inventory, dragged it onto my avatar; the cup attached itself to Marilena's hand. And there the two avs sat companionably, pretending to drink hot coffee while Georgette (actually a bookstore clerk in Scotland) briefed me on the librarian scene on Second Life.

There was more than one library in this virtual world; in fact, the place was bursting with libraries. The Alliance Library System, a real-life consortium in East Peoria, Illinois, had been sponsoring librarian initiatives on Second Life since the spring of 2006, offering information services to avatars and helping libraries and universities gain a foothold. Alliance was helping build virtual libraries all over the place. The best of these, Georgette thought, might be the central library in nineteenth-century Caledon, run by Mr. J. J. Drinkwater. Meanwhile, librarians from the U.S., the U.K., Australia, Canada, China, and multiple European countries (some multilingual, some relying on an imperfect but useful instant translator in Second Life called Babbler) were connecting and collaborating. The Alliance had a vision of all these languages and cultures coming together in the international library, being built on the other side of the island, even as Georgette and Marilena sat nodding their heads on a park bench and this Scottish person and I had a real conversation in the chat box.

What could librarians do in Second Life? They could serve as sources of information about the virtual world, as Georgette had just done. They could help patron-avatars with the mysteries of Second Life. They could research historic sites or eras for people trying to build immersive environments. They could create and furnish buildings on Second Life that they called "libraries," some looking like classic Carnegie libraries from the late nineteenth century, some like futuristic landing pads, all stocked with links to websites and e-books. They could create models of futuristic libraries quickly and cheaply. They could host literary events, book discussion groups, panels, and readings (a surprisingly fun thing to do in Second Life). They could collaborate, share digital resources, and meet. I'm convinced there's no better way to connect with people from far-flung places than on an island in Second Life—it feels like you're all together in one place. The same was true of the parties, where librarians had fun and incidentally gave expression to some of the metaphors of library work—appearing with fairy wings, for instance, or sitting on a chair made of floating books.

Which brings us to the most entertaining thing of all that librarians could do in virtual reality—hang out together. At any hour of the day or night, from any time zone, I could fall in with a group of librarians making a mock video where they danced in sync to an old disco tune, or chatting together in a tree house. Something happened when librarians with digital skills and imagination got together. They invented things. Estimates of the number of librarians on the site were hard to verify, but of the two member groups I followed, one had almost eight hundred members, the other, more than three thousand—plenty to play with, and more than enough for a research-and-development department for the profession, which is what Second Life sometimes seems to be.

And, naturally, librarian-avatars could do what any regular librarian could do: answer our questions.

One night, for instance, I found myself logging into Second Life while at a conference in Alexandria, Virginia. I was nervous about navigating the area the next day and too keyed up to sleep. Three librarian-avatars were hanging around the reference plaza. "Hi, Mari, how's it going?" I told them I was trying to plan my day at the conference, and the concierge was off duty. "We'll help!" they said, and while we gossiped, they also Googled and networked. Within minutes, they gave me directions for negotiating my way via public transportation, advice from a librarian who had made a similar trip, the phone number of a reliable cab company, and the approximate cost of cabfare from the conference site to the train station. They made it easy, erasing my anxiety while arming me cheerfully with information in the middle of the night, for free. "Np," they typed as I teleported away, "no problem."

That's what they did with one hand. With the other, they cooked up crazy library ideas, like Bradburyville, an island where you could take on the form of a character in *Fahrenheit 451* and act out a scene where your home was invaded by "firemen," who confiscated your books and tossed them on a bonfire. I thought of this while reading an interview with Ray Bradbury, *Fahrenheit*'s visionary author and a longtime lover of libraries (though he preferred the computerless model). What would he have made of Bradburyville? He railed about the Internet: "It's distracting," he said. "It's meaningless; it's not real. It's in the air somewhere."

Well, yes . . . but also, no.

There was no nonsense about Hypatia Dejavu. The avatar wore black jeans and sneakers and a white collared shirt, cinched at the waist; white upswept hair framed her chiseled features. Granny glasses perched on her nose, her skin glowed, her gestures were accomplished—from time to time the avatar put her hand on her hips or glanced at her watch, natural-looking movements that had to be scripted or triggered by the human behind her. Everything about her was polished.

In the fall of 2007, Hypatia (and the person behind her) had been on Second Life less than a year, but she clearly had a knack for organizing and exploiting virtual reality. Learning the basics was difficult, she admitted, but soon she was skilled enough to invest in three islands, shape and finish the raw landscape, and build communities. New Boston was dedicated to the New England mystery genre and evoked a moody fishing village, with a graveyard, a haunted house, and a library named for H. P. Lovecraft, complete with exhibits about his life and links to his books. One of the islands was an idealized Florida Key, all sunshine and beachfront; another, Eresos, named for a village in Lesbos, was billed as "The Greek Isles as they never were." Hypatia recovered the fees she paid to Linden Lab by renting out plots to other avatars, many of them librarians. They built houses, furnished and landscaped them, entertained within them. They were all rated

Mature, a warning that one might encounter half-naked avatars spouting X-rated text. "I don't do PG," she told me.

Her competence extended to her profession. She was a recent graduate of an online master's course in library science, so she quickly took charge of the reference desk on Info Island.

"I've got a passion for reference service," Hypatia typed in our chat box, "so that's what I wanted to do here, but the person in charge never responded, and there seemed to be no schedule. So I started to fill in the gaps. After a few weeks, I learned that (1) I was doing more time than anyone else there, and (2) the person running reference had disappeared." The virtual Alliance Library System, funded by the Illinois consortium, was growing quickly; an expert, confident volunteer was just what they needed. The directors invited Hypatia to be their head of reference services. "It's difficult to lead in this environment with all volunteers, but over ten months, we've gone from about eight volunteers covering sixteen hours a week to forty-two covering about ninety-two hours." Because she compiled statistics, she knew that approximately two-thirds of her volunteers had a master's degree in library and information science; the rest she personally trained. Most of the questions they answered were about Second Life. Reference service for avatars more than quadrupled under her direction—impressive, considering that she managed all this organizing after work.

Hypatia's profile noted that she was lesbian and partnered, but as with many of the librarians I met in virtual reality, her real-life identity was a secret. Her employer at an unnamed public library in Pennsylvania was "openly hostile" to Second Life. (I assumed the objection was not to the library activities on the site but to its reputation for risqué sex scenes.) So Hypatia practiced strict compartmentalization. She never went on Second Life at work, and once online, she separated work from play; like her virtual staff, she maintained a relatively conservative professional image while on duty. I didn't really care who operated the controls behind Hypatia or what she did on her virtual Greek island. The spirit of an ambitious and influential librarian was expressed in that avatar, and she could teach me plenty.

"By its nature our project here is focused on events, displays and directing people toward deeper resources," Hypatia was explaining. "Would you like to see?" Then she led me toward the brand-new Alliance virtual library, set for its grand opening in a couple of days. That is, she tried to lead me—my avatar got stuck in a walking animation and my application crashed. Damn!

It was my first formal interview on Second Life, and don't ask me why I picked such a formidable character. Not trusting my usual Internet connection, or my family to leave me in peace, I'd driven to the Chappaqua library and reserved one of the two private study rooms; I had my laptop and power cord, an electric outlet, a strong wireless signal, and a cup of real coffee. Unfortunately, I spaced out about the fact that the library closed at eight p.m., so if the interview went longer than an hour, I was sunk. Technically, interviewing on Second Life is a lot like juggling. I had to maneuver my avatar while typing all my questions and comments into the chat box—and if I wanted to quote Hypatia accurately, I had to simultaneously take notes with a pencil and paper (there were ways to save chat logs from Second Life but I hadn't yet figured them out). And then there were the vagaries of this gazillion-gigabyte application, the crashes, glitches, and lags, which all participants experienced to some degree. So, yeah, I was sweating.

Hypatia was waiting in the library plaza when I logged back on, and led Marilena briskly toward the new library. The Alliance Virtual Library had several open doors and windows around all sides. Unlike the brick-and-mortar libraries with their narrow and controlled entrances, the better to protect the valuable resources within, virtual libraries tended to be porous, open, and airy, easy for avatars to fly into. This one had two floors and was divided into neat, themed sections. *Digital Collections* had tables set with pictures of computers; with a simple right-click, you could link to Project Gutenberg and its thirty thousand free downloadable books, or to the Internet Public Library, a juicy website full of resources supplied by a network of busy digital librarians. *Serials* had kiosks where you could download copies of more than a dozen magazines or newspapers produced specifically for Second Life residents—*The Metaverse Messenger, sLiterary, The Second Life Herald* ("always fairly unbalanced"). Clicking on a display would bring you either a notecard, which you could keep in your inventory and read at your leisure, or a link to a webpage that opened in a separate window on your screen. Hypatia was especially proud of the *Human Sexuality* section, which she built from scratch to provide links to resources for every variation of sexual preference (or the thinking pornographer), from *Abstinence Clearinghouse* to *Savage Love*.

"One nice thing about virtual services is that we're able to discuss things openly that would often cause problems otherwise," Hypatia observed. "There's a very large gay, lesbian, bisexual and transsexual population on Second Life." In *Coming of Age in Second Life: An Anthropologist Explores the Virtually Human*, Tom Boellstorff confessed, "I could have written an entire book on queer Second Life—which, as one resident noted is 'queer along axes we don't even have in first life.'"

I'm guessing the librarian behind Hypatia had lost a few battles bringing such resources to her public library. She named her avatar after Hypatia of Alexandria, a fourth-century librarian, scholar, and pagan, torn to death by a Christian mob.

We teleported upstairs and checked out the other collections, among them *Romance* and *Cowboy and Western*, with its links to cowboy movies and poetry sites. The roof was open, so we flew up and out.

"Info International," Hypatia began typing, "is designed to be a cultural hub and the heart of a growing Info Island archipelago." Along with the library, other sites slated to open on the island included a Mexican cantina, a Chinese café and education center (staffed with Chinese-speakers), and a garden. There would also be a suspension bridge dedicated to stateless people around the world, featuring links to notecards every few steps with information about the Roma Gypsies, say, or the hill tribe people of Thailand.

Hypatia wanted to show me the bridge, which she'd programmed, but it was closing time at the brick-and-mortar library in Chappaqua. I ran out of the study room with my laptop, and thrust it at Cathy, who was on the reference desk. On my screen, Marilena and Hypatia hovered like Tinker Bells above the virtual library. I explained that one of these avatars was a librarian and one was, more or less, me, and that I was in the middle of an interview. Could I possibly stay past closing? "Will you look at that!" Cathy marveled and called another librarian over. Together, they gaped at my screen. "That's a librarian?"

Cathy said there was a program going on next door in the auditorium, which the wireless network covered; I could sit in the hall outside, then exit through the auditorium when I was done. So I hurried over and flopped down on the carpet like a college student. The computer was hot on my lap; heat radiated from my body. Marilena was bouncing off the virtual library wall. But Hypatia looked as cool and composed as ever, hand on her hip and eye on her watch.

The speed with which the information archipelago in Second Life was growing was crazy-making. Every time I ran off to chase a real-world librarian, one or more virtual libraries opened. Just days after Hypatia took me touring, the Info International compound debuted with speeches in English and Chinese, games, prizes, a dance, and virtual fireworks. Virtual fireworks! Who, I wondered, thought up such marvels? My screen exploded with graceful arcs of color. Standing in-world as Marilena, with my new long red hair and dressed in another great new outfit, while also lying around in person in my rumpled bed in an old nightgown, I watched the glorious bursts of color from both perspectives, and tried once more to interest my husband in the spectacles of Second Life. "Yes, yes, but what's it *for*?" he said, as he always does.

Every few weeks, another meticulously created environment debuted with parties, tours, and celebrations. The loose network of volunteers jumped on every new idea with speed and intensity, and real-world grants (from the Alliance Library System in Illinois, or Linden Labs, or from commercial sponsors and library vendors) often drove the antic schedule. In late October, a call for volunteers went up on the Alliance's electronic bulletin board. Did anyone want to help create the Land of Lincoln? By January, final touches were being put on an expansive region that encompassed a virtual, historically accurate, 1860s-era White House, replete with period furniture; a Civil War graveyard; a Union encampment; the village of Lincolnshire, along with its library, general store, one-room schoolhouse, church, town hall, and livery repair; Abe's Springfield home, re-created from the original plans; and a plantation like the one where Mary Todd Lincoln spent her early life.

The Land of Lincoln was dense and deep; everything you clicked brought up cards of information, or linked to digital collections about cooking in the 1860s . . . period music . . .

the founding of the Lincoln-Herndon law offices . . . popular novels of the era . . . cartoons of Lincoln that had appeared in the London *Punch*. Every aspect reflected hours of research done by librarians who had not only tapped a network of their peers (in their real and second lives) to verify each physical detail, but had also corralled collections that could be accessed from the Land of Lincoln. Soon, for instance, the Joseph N. Nathanson Collection of Lincolniana at McGill University would be accessible through the virtual library, thanks to a McGill graduate student in library and information science who was active in Second Life.

The slave quarters behind Mary's Grove Plantation constituted a history course on their own. Think of Colonial Williamsburg, set during the Civil War and shrunk to your laptop. The cluster of simple log buildings were designed and furnished according to the accounts of real slaves. Outside one dwelling stood images of six upright books, each linked to the full e-book text, as well as critical commentary—including *The Narrative of Sojourner Truth* and W. E. B. Du Bois's *The Souls of Black Folk* ("being a problem is a strange experience—peculiar even for one who has never been anything else"). Interviews with actual slaves could be read directly from a larger open book resting on a pedestal; its pages turned with a mouse click. Notes and links to sites about Abolition and Emancipation were cleverly woven into the scene; a Web source about the Underground Railroad popped up when you clicked a patchwork quilt stretched between cabins. The slave cabins, created by librarians with the Second Life names of Daisyblue Hefferman and Pipsqueak Fiddlesticks, represented one small plot in a historic simulation that was compiled in people's free time in a speedy few months.

I know, I know . . . These hardworking librarians put together this serious, interactive, imaginative 3-D exhibit, but their names were *Daisyblue Hefferman* and *Pipsqueak Fiddlesticks*. It presented a problem. I attended a lecture in Second Life by Daisyblue and noticed that the whiteboard on which she flashed pictures of Land of Lincoln had been designed by AngryBeth Shortbread. The names were the essence of Second Life humor, a fusion of whimsy and attitude. Zen-Mondo Wormser! Perplexity Peccable! One avatar admired mine, Marilena Basevi; she thought it made a great name for a spy—which, in a way, I was. For a while, library conferences that offered presentations on virtual and avatar librarianship featured both the real world and Second Life names of the presenters, as when Barbara Galik/Puglet Dancer spoke at the Computers in Libraries conference in 2008. The silliness of the names was a barrier, though, and guaranteed that anybody coming to listen would walk in with a smirk. At any rate, I noticed that at later conferences, presenters on virtual-world issues were identified only by their tamer real names.

The grand opening on the long Presidents' Day weekend in 2008 featured a formal ball with appearances by a virtual Mrs. Lincoln and Abraham Lincoln, who waltzed with Marilena, apologized for his dancing skills, and told her, "I have never studied the art of paying compliments to women; but I must say that if all that has been said by orators and poets since the creation of the world in praise of women were applied to the women of America, it would not do them justice." (He didn't step on Marilena's feet, of course; his avatar, just like mine, had been scripted and animated to dance exquisitely.) He regretted that we could share only one waltz; "many women and just one president," he murmured. I was charmed.

Lori Bell, who worked for the Alliance Library System in Illinois and was one of the propelling forces behind its pioneering stake in Second Life, felt a responsibility to bring to fruition anything her librarian-volunteers dreamed up. Her avatar, Lorelei Junot, was a fairy godmother, giving away plots of virtual land to any real-world librarian who promised to build a virtual library. Bell had learned about Second Life in early 2006 and leapt immediately. Her title in the Illinois consortium was director of innovation, and obviously, here was something innovative: every time she visited, she saw Second Life being created. It was immediately obvious to her that she and her colleagues could bring something to this interactive world, participate in its invention, and develop a whole new arena to promote the image of librarians.

So Bell bought an island in the Alliance's name, set up a virtual reference desk, and began the first collaborative library project in Second Life. She got her friend Barbara Galik, an academic librarian at Bradley University and president of the Alliance's board of directors, to sign up as well. Galik developed her avatar, the knockout Puglet Dancer, then bought two of her staff members new computers to entice them onto Second Life.

Rhonda Trueman, an academic librarian at Johnson & Wales University in Charlotte, North Carolina, got into Second Life with her husband and daughter after reading a story in *BusinessWeek*, also in early 2006. As soon as she discovered Bell's reference desk, she knew she had to get involved. She fashioned a sweet-looking librarian-avatar named Abbey Zenith and threw herself into volunteering, bringing such energy and imagination to her tasks that the Alliance hired her part-time; that is, a consortium in Illinois paid U.S. dollars to the librarian Rhonda Trueman for the work she did as a librarian-avatar. Two years later, Trueman and Lori Bell collaborated to edit the book *Virtual Worlds, Real Libraries*, and with Galik and a host of others have expanded library services in Second Life; the count in mid-2009 was 128 virtual libraries in this system, from Bradley University's replica of its campus library to IBM's corporate library.

Junot, Bell, Trueman, Galik, Hypatia Dejavu—none of them predicted the explosive growth of the library scene here. "This started as a small pilot project and grew faster and wilder than we could keep up with," Bell explained. "My ambition is to keep my head above water."

Each success made them bolder. The Alliance in Second Life offered noncredit courses in virtual librarianship through the University of Illinois at Urbana-Champaign and conducted educational and literary conferences in Second Life. It also started a group within the American Library Association to explore ways to formalize the field of virtual librarianship. New librarians entering Second Life and getting drunk on the creative possibilities were warned of the biggest pitfalls, like the resistance of their actual library colleagues and directors. "We have had librarians nearly lose their job over participating," said Trueman. Almost as lethal to new volunteers was the unintended consequence of all that creative stimulation: it was just so exciting to be a librarian with an avatar and an imagination, you couldn't stop building libraries and curating exhibits. You burned out.

> For, you see, so many out-of-the-way things had happened lately, that Alice had begun to think that very few things indeed were really impossible.
>
> —*Alice's Adventures in Wonderland*

Marilena materialized under a gazebo in the square in Caledon's Victoria City. Where exactly was she? Coordinates 127, 128, 24 on the Second Life grid, near a sign that said: "Welcome to 19th Century Steampunk Victorian Caledon." The square was surrounded by gas lamps and what looked like stately bank buildings of a certain era. Inside each storefront: antiques for sale, dresses with bustles, rimless eyeglasses, spats—or rather, virtual representations of such items. A few carts parked on the square displayed gift boxes with things free or almost free: top hats, archaeology tools from the Royal

Society, and steampunk goggles for avatars: images of the detritus of a previous century, polished and repurposed for the avatars of the twenty-first century.

A half-cat, half-human avatar emerged from the mist by the locomotive tracks to ask if the traveler needed assistance.

Well, yes. The traveler certainly did. Marilena was in a place that felt familiar but was in fact twenty thousand leagues deep into the weird: the past, complete with its vision of the future, as imagined in the present, and populated by cartoons.

We were searching for the Caledon library and its chief librarian, Mr. J. J. Drinkwater. Ah, said the half-furry thing, Drinkwater was an elusive and shy personage. Maintained a colony for homeless librarians. A credit to Caledon. (Did everyone in Caledon talk like this? Yes, and so did I when Marilena was on the scene—the urge to speak somewhat pompously in the "sim" was contagious.) The guide pointed a paw to an alley with the library tucked behind, and urged Marilena to pick up a free bustle dress to wear while wandering around, just to get in the spirit of things. So I scored a long dove-gray gown with layers of folds and frills for Marilena, and a fetching felt hat, and, transformed, commenced snooping.

The whimsical country of Caledon epitomized the more civilized side of Second Life. It was a world both fussy and playful, and it occupied a significant cultural corner of virtual reality; estimates of its citizenry run upwards of eight hundred (out of roughly thirty thousand to sixty thousand citizens logged on to the whole of Second Life anytime I jumped in, most of them, according to the rankings of popular sites, seeking warplay or sex). The library anchored and helped define the Caledon community, collecting bibliographic material about the nineteenth century, steampunk (the future as imagined by Victorians like H. G. Wells and Jules Verne), and imagined history. It also hosted "exhibits, book talks, lectures, and the occasional donnybrook." J.J. had twice been challenged to haiku duels and turned them into fund-raising events (he won both). The notecard that described the library elucidated: "This site draws its name from the Chivalric Order of the Duchy of Caledon Primverness, and Members of the Order take vows of Literacy, Obstinacy, and Bibliomancy." *Bibliomancy?* It's defined for us a little further down: "Divination by jolly well Looking It Up."

At any rate, there was no one there to look anything up. J. J. Drinkwater was offline, said a little sign in front. Through a comfy reading room (if you clicked on one of the balls, nestled like a pillow in the chairs, your avatar would sit down and seem to be reading a book), a replica of a circulation desk stood with an odd device on top, a brass contraption with a piece of paper in its jaws, and a domed top with some melted-looking alphabet keys. "Touch here to leave a message," it said. Marilena touched it, and the odd machine flashed a prompt on my screen: "Leave a one-line message after the beep . . . BEEP!" I left a message for J.J.

So much for the clever gadgets of Caledon: The message never reached him. Or perhaps the shy librarian was hiding. I resolved to track him down at one of the events that occurred continually throughout Caledon, many sponsored by his very own self. And soon enough I did.

The Alice in Wonderland Tea was preceded by three days of *Alice's Adventures in Wonderland* and *Through the Looking-Glass* read aloud over Radio Riel, the Internet radio station that could be streamed in or out of Second Life. I listened to the reading while browsing a virtual nineteenth-century store for the right floaty gown, period boots, and long gloves, then made Marilena up like a grand titled lady while listening to the part where Alice introduces the Cheshire Cat ("'I don't like the look of it at all,' said the King: 'however, it may kiss my hand, if it likes'").

Arriving at the green in Caledon, I felt I had stumbled on a country wedding in an Austen novel. Folks in period costumes converged from every direction, greeting each other and being welcomed in courtly fashion by the librarian. Some avatars appeared as Alice, the Cheshire Cat, the Queen of Hearts, or the Dormouse—and not simply costumed as these characters, either; they *were* these creatures. Alice looked like a blond girl in a pinafore; the Dormouse was a miniature *furry*, as the animal avatars are called on Second Life. J. J. Drinkwater sported a stunning suit and duster with a lofty top hat crowning his mild, friendly face and round, rimless glasses perched on his nose. He led us ceremoniously to a green space behind the clock tower where a long table was set with cakes and teapots, and there he conjured up chairs. Once the twenty or so avatars had taken seats, the tableau looked altogether like a crackpot tea party. Exactly!

The conversation, conducted by the people behind the avatars, unscrolled in a chatlog. It blended erudite wit with sublime goofiness and played out in a headlong rush; at least three discussions seemed to be happening concurrently. While J.J. and several others talked about the mathematical puzzles embedded in Lewis Carroll's books, exclamations of "Off with their heads!" and other spirited interjections peppered the chat. Occasionally, someone would drop the charade, as when one of the avatars "realizes how silly a gargoyle discussing literature is."

I was too overcome by the speed and non-sequiturial madness of it all to add much; instead, I sat meekly on my stool at home, while Marilena daintily lifted teacup to mouth and looked perfectly at ease at the banquet table on the lawn, surrounded by the plumed citizens of Caledon. In real time, it was Sunday afternoon in my kitchen in New York, and my real children kept coming in to pop soda cans and ask what was for dinner. "Shhh! I'm working!" I said, and they rolled their eyes. "Sure you are."

"Nonsense requires sense," one gentleman was declaring as I snapped back to attention, just in time for the discussion about the hookah and the stoned caterpillar and a few disparaging remarks about the novel's unsatisfying ending. "Ooh . . . that provokes me no end, that ending does," one avatar summed up.

"What a lovely party," chattered another. "More cake, anyone?"

On the one hand, people who had read the Alice books multiple times, had consulted the annotated edition, and referred to Lewis Carroll as Dodgson (his actual name) were having a real, if fractured, discussion in an unusual setting; on the other hand, the puns and jokes and sly references to the oddity of the scene were pure lark. Second Life, which made the magical aspects of our actions seem ordinary, was the ideal place to discuss *Alice's Adventures in Wonderland*. A chair appeared out of thin air each time another guest arrived. The teapots were filled with endless tea; the cakes multiplied instead of diminished. The Dormouse and the other creatures spoke. And wisps of wordplay and poetry echoed after the last guest teleported away—*that provokes me no end, that ending does . . .*

I'll go out on a limb here. It was the most fun I'd ever had at a library event.

In the blunter, more prosaic, other world—the "aetheric world," as Caledonians call it—J. J. Drinkwater was J. J. Jacobson, an itinerant librarian just shy of fifty, a former catalog and metadata specialist who left a real job to spend time cultivating library skills in the metaverse. Jacobson seemed to live from couch to couch, L.A., San Francisco, Seattle, a small town in Idaho, Ann Arbor—friends in every port, and enough consulting work to keep going. A previous career as chef served as backup, and culinary librarianship was an enduring interest.

But the bottom line was: "I left a faculty position in an academic library to do this full time."

We met in Caledon at the library, formally known as the Jack and Elaine Whitehorn Library. The Whitehorns were the real life parents of the library's benefactor, a Caledon resident who had a vision of an intellectual center and had appealed to the Alliance for a suitable head librarian. J.J. had just been raving to someone there about Caledon. So J.J. got the job, helped build the library, and found a central role for it in this already-thriving community.

J.J. firmly believed that "Libraries need to leverage every technological capacity we can . . . and we need to learn how to serve an expanding range of kinds of communities." The Alliance virtual libraries are playgrounds for librarians and wonderful places to hold classes and events, but Caledon had something they didn't: an active group of patrons, an organic virtual community. After Masterpiece Theatre ran a series of films based on Jane Austen novels, Caledonians flocked to this library for lively discussions; storytelling sessions and dress-up balls abounded. The haiku duels were wildly popular, and the librarian is something of a celebrity there, "a trophy librarian," J.J. conceded.

I complimented him on the Alice in Wonderland tea, and he bowed from the waist, and said, "One reason to be a librarian in Second Life is that it is such a world where even serious professionals may frolic."

He was dressed in an anachronistic uniform with ruffles and purple cuffs, and boots that a Hessian soldier might have worn clomping off to war. From time to time a large ledger appeared in his avatar's hand and he busily made an entry. There was a half-smile on J.J.'s avatar face that periodically expanded to a full Cheshire.

Standing around the lovely library with its cozy wood furniture and rotunda structure, and gazing at the current exhibit—" 'How like an angel!': Depicting Male Beauty in Word and Image," which, among other portraits, included one of J. J. Drinkwater himself—we discussed the finer points of J.J.'s clever animations, and the distinctions between the librarian and the librarian-avatar. "J.J.'s real name is in the profile because I felt Caledon deserved to know that it had a real librarian running its library. Anyone can call themselves anything here. It leads to immense chicanery, both commercial and intellectual."

I agreed; and to small chicanery, too. I was thinking of the gulf between my appearance and my beauteous avatar's when I asked if J. J. Drinkwater looked like J. J. Jacobson. There was a moment of confusion, then J.J.'s face changed a bit on my screen and the short dark hair, with little sprouts of bangs on either side of the forehead, turned into a long mane of brown hair, the top strands pulled back in a distinctly more feminine style. "This is closer," J.J. said, and I thought, "Whoa! Who is this nineteenth-century gentleman? A candid fellow—though not, perhaps, a fellow?" "Cool," I said, and, completely flustered, leapt right over the whole matter.

Then we embarked on a field trip to see some of the branch libraries of Caledon that have appeared thanks to J.J.'s inspi-

ration and encouragement. I was particularly enchanted by
the one in Tinyville, built for miniature avatars (usually fur-
ries in the shape of animals like badgers or penguins). There
were stores that sell avatars, along with hundreds of outfits,
costumes, and props, and now there was also a library, with
a low door, miniature chairs, and, inside, digital collections
consisting of links to stories about short things, like children
and short fiction. There was even a link to the Wizard of Oz
exhibit at the Library of Congress, a nod, no doubt, to the
Munchkins. The library was set on a street of tiny buildings.
A miniature blacksmith shop next door, set in an old tree
trunk, had a fire burning inside. The whole neighborhood
was set in a jewel of a forest. I felt like we were in a fairy tale.
J.J. and Marilena stood on the sidewalk for a while, chatting. J.J. taught classes in virtual librarianship for the Alliance,
and used one of his "alts" (short for alternative avatars) as a
teaching assistant. "I don't get the alts," I told him. "How
does that work? How can you have more than one avatar
going at once?"

J.J. could bring up Second Life on two windows on his
laptop, "and I sometimes run one on the laptop and one on the
desktop," J.J. explained. "I have a friend here who tells me she
can run *four* Second Life clients at once, on her laptop. Shall
I show you?" Soon the little sidewalk was crowded as we were
joined by a tiny lisping ferret ("the wibwarian of Cawedon,
Mr. Dwinkwater") and Cuthbert Snook, a tall, bald male in
a Renaissance doublet over tights. Everyone there, except me,
was an incarnation of J.J.

"I think you're probably familiar with the way certain authors fission themselves off into two 'voices' and argue with themselves? Yeats, I think, in some of his poetry. Wittgenstein, certainly. Well, here you can do it literally. I can let Snook be one part of myself and this ferret be another, and converse with myself. Which, of course, we do all the time, no?"

The ferret scooted off. Cuthbert bowed and offered to dance, and twirled me around the sidewalk in front of Tinyville, while the librarian in the purple-frilled jacket, long hair cascading over his shoulders, stood by, smiling and making occasional notations in an old ledger.

Craig Anderson (also known as as Draconius Merlin) wore a fedora and stood on a street corner outside a popular bar in Center City, Philadelphia, as promised. Like Steven Harris (Stolvano Barbosa), who showed up on the corner, too, his human form was tall, cute, outgoing, and a bit fey—a library guy. Anderson welcomed me and the woman I knew as Ms. Q., who appeared at the Alliance parties in Second Life in the form of a fox avatar, and we were joined by Jeremy Kemp (Jeremy Kabumpo), who trained his San Jose State students in the fine points of virtual reality, then hired them to design and rebuild the ALA's island on Second Life. We were all waved into the bar and, disguised as mere humans, settled upstairs among the young professionals of Philadelphia. A pink-cheeked woman interrupted us before the bruschetta came. "I hope this doesn't sound odd, but I'm looking for some people

I know but haven't met." And so another librarian in both real and Second life squeezed into the booth.

We were attending the ALA's mid-winter conference in Philadelphia, January 2008, where the exhilarating first meeting of the member-initiated group Virtual Communities and Libraries had just taken place. Librarians had been slow to jump into the Web in the early days; they wouldn't make that mistake again. They took pride in the fact that they were early adopters of any number of technological innovations, particularly virtual worlds, and the room where they met that afternoon was crackling with something I'd rarely seen in a librarian gathering—palpable excitement. I had sat next to Joe Sanchez, a young linebacker-sized librarian from the University of Texas at Austin, who was conducting ambitious research projects in Second Life with his library science students. We traded notes, and he showed me his maxed-out MacBook Pro. "It's a little hot-rod," he bragged.

Now the wine flowed and giddiness took over. "Who else have you met?" everyone wanted to know. One of the assembled had attended the Internet Librarian conference in Monterey, California, and met J. J. Drinkwater. "And he's just as courtly and gracious a gentleman as he is in Second Life." There were many exclamations of admiration for J.J. and the community he has helped foster online. "But isn't J.J. a she?" I said. "Oh, no!" I was told, forcefully. Had I misread J.J.'s transformation?

Kemp ran off to find us a bigger and more comfortable spot,

and called minutes later; he was down an alley off Spruce, at a Tudor-style bar with a great long table like something from *Beowulf*. Rhonda Trueman (Abbey Zenith) and others were waiting there. Another crackpot tea party, this one with humans.

We ordered food and wine and drank toasts to the avatar-friends who couldn't join us for this jolly evening, like Lori Bell, who would have loved to hear her efforts praised in person but was sidelined with a sprained ankle. The bar began filling up with other patrons, the noise level rose. I realized something was strange when I went to look for the ladies' room: there wasn't a ladies' room. The waiter grabbed my hand—"No trough for you, darling!"—and led me through a serving station to a broom closet with a toilet. When I rejoined the table and looked around, I saw only men at the other tables and on the bar stools, and a transvestite lurching past on high heels. I caught Trueman's eye. "I was wondering when someone was going to notice," she drawled.

It was all . . . well, forgive me, but it seemed like a scene from Second Life.

In the alley afterward, we milled around the steps of the bar, loath to end the fun. One of them grabbed my sleeve, the one who had so firmly set me straight about the great librarian of Caledon.

"You were right about J.J.," I was told. "But we never say that. Ever."

All right. Deep breath. J. J. Drinkwater, the avatar, was clearly a mister. But J. J. Jacobson? For two years I had e-mailed and chatted with the librarian via computer without knowing, or feeling the need to know, the "real" sex of my correspondent. When I absolutely had to have a pronoun, I wrote Jacobson directly, who fired back a joke: "Mixed. Or the increasingly popular 'It's Complicated,' " then relented and gave me what I needed—a pronoun. In this case, a *she*.

"It's Complicated" is much more interesting than *she*, but I can't get hung up on this. What's important is not which pronoun gets attached to this librarian, but what she has done. Jacobson has created a librarian-avatar who is not only useful to the community but also emblematic of its patrons' intellectual aspirations, and a badge of civilized, even courtly, discourse—a status symbol that demonstrates the value they placed on literature and history.

J. J. Jacobson had teamed up with another librarian from Second Life to make a presentation at the ALA annual conference in 2008. "Those who stopped by were most interested and curious," she told me afterward, "but the thing our visitors had the hardest time wrapping their heads around was that our libraries are not the in-world presence of some brick-and-mortar library but have an independent existence."

It was hard to fathom that you could go to the *Human Sexuality* collection in the Alliance Virtual Library and immediately have at your fingertips the distilled resources of the Web on the topic of gender; or that the most useful collection of instant reference sources, from dictionaries to news outlets, had been gathered by Rhonda Trueman at the plaza on Info Island. These *collections*—assembled, defined, and used within Second Life—shared the additional advantage of the real-life library: they existed in a community of patrons and librarians. It's just that the Second Life patrons and librarians happened to look like Miss Universe, Fritz the Cat, Mr. Clean in Renaissance garb, and Prospector Pete.

There were several academic degrees in J. J. Jacobson's pocket, including a master's in information science, and an endless enthusiasm for librarianship. But what made her special was an aspect of the job that is not much called for in a brick-and-mortar setting, though it can make or break a librarian in Second Life. "Harmless role-playing" was how she described it. "If I talk to people in a serious and encouraging way about their research interests, and if I can get excited and find them resources, that invites them further into their research. I try to get them to volunteer for the Caledon library. I notice I can make them feel that they have something to bring to Caledon. That goes hand in hand with what a community library can do: reflect back to a community its culture, show them how rich it is, and how they're connected—which is what archives have always done: they show a society its culture, its heritage. They say *this is who you are.*"

Got that? J. J. Drinkwater is the metaphor and front man for an active librarian who researches and creates exhibits, conducts book discussions, and serves patrons, just like a regular librarian, though with an exaggerated flourish. Behind the scenes, while busy with bibliographies and programs and consultations with colleagues in various real-world work spaces, the real librarian keeps her computer screen open to Second

Life and Drinkwater's Caledon office, a glassed-in aerie furnished with an antique desk and tools. It acts as her visual wallpaper. "Somehow it's a great environment for working." She has almost daily conversations with her frequent collaborator, Gabrielle Riel of Radio Riel. "Her human and my human talk on the phone." The librarian and the radio director are "two small business owners, trying to run professional-style businesses on people's TV time." Jacobson admitted there might come a day when she would move on from Second Life, though I couldn't picture it. There were other virtual worlds out there, and still more in the planning stages. For a while, there was a prototype of a virtual world of Shakespeare. "My God, a virtual world of Shakespeare!" Jacobson enthused. "'If it were now to die / 'Twere now to be most happy'!"

Meanwhile, when a full-time consulting job in Ann Arbor sidelined Jacobson briefly, she complained that "trying to run an imaginary library is kicking my pixilated butt with a pixilated shoe." But she knew that I knew that she was joking about that "imaginary."

Dave Mewhinney told me he was sick. I had talked to him many times in his avatar forms: as Haldin Koba, holding court at Info Plaza or the librarian parties, and as Lena Kjeller, in a bustle and lace-up boots, pointing proudly to the billboard that proclaimed her volunteer librarian of the month. Mewhinney's wife, Holly Peters (her avatar was Hollyjean, the Infomaniac and ebullient hostess), had dragged him onto Second Life shortly after his diagnosis. The couple had been looking for cancer resources when they stumbled on the reference librarians on Info Island. Within months, Mewhinney had thrown himself into reference work, meeting Hypatia Dejavu's exacting standards and putting his time and research skills to satisfying use. Then the Deadwood sim opened, and Mewhinney discovered his inner Lena. The last few times we met, we talked about Deadwood and its library. I was going to visit the historic sim, dress in frontier costume, and sit with Lena Kjellar at the library for an afternoon. Perhaps one of the Deadwood residents, pretending to be illiterate, would wander in and ask the librarian to look something up. That would have been sweet.

But late in 2008, Peters sent word that her husband had been hospitalized and was in intensive care. The cancer he'd managed for two and a half years was no longer responding to treatment. One of the Second Life librarians organized a site near the reference plaza dedicated to Haldin/Lena, where we could leave messages and gifts, so Peters could take a laptop into his hospital room and show him the best wishes and farewells from his many friends.

I called him a friend twice, as Haldin and as Lena, the way social networking sites have you "friend" each other to be in the same network. He and Lena were valuable sources, and I was fascinated by Mewhinney's story. It's funny, isn't it, that an older man, an electrical engineer and railroad freak with a basement of model trains, could turn himself into a frontier librarian, complete with curls and a bustled gown? And not just because a twenty-first-century male engineer was inhabiting the skirts and spirit of a nineteenth-century female librarian. Mewhinney had turned his search for health information into a position on a triple frontier—in the fictional frontier library of Deadwood, on the frontier of Second Life, and at the front of cyber-librarianship.

Surreal as it seemed, the digital avatars, Lena and Haldin, would die along with the man who animated them—evidence that the virtual world is also real and, however malleable, subject to some of the same, distressingly real, limitations.

10.

GOTHAM CITY

In the first decade of the twenty-first century, at the inter-section of rapid change and financial meltdown, some of its librarians carve out a niche, some get iced out, and some help plan the future of the libraries and how we use them.

David Smith used to recognize writers when he worked at the beautiful old Doubleday Bookstore on Fifth Avenue. He remembered spotting J. Anthony Lukas, author of *Common Ground* and other award-winning political books. When a job in the periodicals department opened up at the New York Public Library, the big marble edifice with the lions in front, Smith took it, then earned a master's degree in his spare time and became a librarian. One day Smith was at his post at the reference desk, a burnished-wood structure that lends all business conducted there a solemn importance, when J. Anthony Lukas approached and gave him a call slip.

This library is huge. It encompasses two city blocks, millions of items, miles of shelves, hundreds of librarians, a cavernous storage space beneath Bryant Park, the whole thing humming like a freeway. You locate what you want in the digital catalog, an ever-expanding index of knowledge. You write down your name and the particulars of the item, its call number and title, on an old-fashioned copy slip with a stubby pencil. You have just used the most sophisticated tool in the library and the least sophisticated; the twenty-first-century library embraces both. Smith, or another reference librarian, checks the call number against a map of the library, tucks the slip into one of the 1911-era brass tubes, and sends your request whizzing through pneumatic pipes to a station deep in the building's bowels. If you're lucky, the book is where it is supposed to be and arrives at the call desk on a conveyer belt; the slip you sent out like a prayer is answered. If the gods aren't smiling, or your request is incomplete, you get your slip handed back to you.

Lukas could untangle the complications of the desegregation conflict in 1960s and '70s Boston and tease out stories from the secretive Nixon White House, but he couldn't get the book he wanted from the NYPL. Smith returned his slip with an apology and explained what was missing from his request. "What's wrong? Jesus! One more thing!" the writer muttered as he walked away—so the librarian recalls. "The guy always seemed down." Smith kicks himself every time he thinks about it. Two years later, Lukas died, a suicide. Surely the failure to obtain a library book isn't grounds for despair, but "if it were today," Smith vowed. "I'd go and find the book myself."

It was his first inkling that writers needed special attention, but at the time, Smith was too young and shy to introduce himself. Later, as a seasoned librarian, he used what he called his "radar for writers" and swooped in immediately. He saw a prominent critic, standing in line with a cane, ushered him to a table, and personally delivered his books. If Smith thought he recognized a name, he Googled it to make sure, then pressed his business card into their hands. "Let me know if I can do anything to help," he'd say.

A guy in his fifties in rimless glasses and a pullover sweater, Smith seemed like a throwback. He hunt-and-pecked on the keyboard; he didn't care about blogs or any of that virtual-world stuff. It annoyed him when the NYPL software migrated and wiped out all his old e-mails; that was his filing system for his correspondence. "I don't even know what *migration* means," he grumbled.

But Smith was an indefatigable reference librarian whose skills were particularly suited to this transitional age. He was expert at navigating online sources, and he could wring things out of Google that I couldn't find. And if the digital catalog said something wasn't in the library, well, he always regarded the digital catalog as a work-in-progress and checked a print source to back it up, like the eight-hundred-volume "black book catalog," a compilation of the laboriously copied images of the old NYPL card catalog. He searched everything.

A few years ago, historian James W. Cook was trying to compile a P. T. Barnum reader and was hunting the holy grail of Barnum scholarship—the last few chapters of Barnum's semiautobiographical novella, *Adventures of an Adventurer*, which had appeared in serial newspaper installments in the old *New York Atlas*. The 1841 issues of the paper had disappeared from libraries, but Cook sent a query to the NYPL reference desk just in case. After checking the library's online catalog, Smith combed the "black book," finding a reference to the paper that hadn't made it into the digital record. He located the newspapers in storage, where they had been "forgotten and invisible, for almost a century," as Cook wrote subsequently in *The Colossal P. T. Barnum Reader*. Smith called the historian when he found them. "You just made my book," Cook told him.

Smith became so identified as the writers' librarian that he was profiled in the *New York Times* in late 2007 as "The Library's Helpful Sage of the Stacks." He was pictured beaming up from his desk, tucked in a cubby behind the reference area in the Bill Blass Catalog Room, surrounded by a mess of books and papers and a fringe of Post-it notes. An eclectic ring of books had been planted like flags around the top of his partition, the work of some of the writers he had helped: James Brady, Edna O'Brien, Daniel Okrent, David Halberstam, and a host of the less well known.

Smith read them all. He read everything he could by the writers he helped, recommending their books to others, even buying secondhand copies to pass out to friends and random readers. He'd tell the story of any of these books to anyone, the story the book itself told—"It's fantastic. You've got to read it!"—and the meta-story of how he had intersected with it, helped the author find something, or came in on his day off to help pull research. He'd pick up one of these books to read aloud a great passage, or show off the line where he was thanked in the acknowledgments. "'The *peerless* David Smith,'" he'd say with relish.

The old Smith had been a bookstore clerk and then a librarian just going through the motions, a man who read for escape and who let even the writers he recognized pass by unacknowledged. Then he became part of the process. The authors whose work ended up on the shelves of his library were all around him, absorbing what had already been written and turning it into something new. He saw them getting intimidated, frustrated. The library, its online catalog, the profusion of databases, the protocols—it was complicated. They were on deadline. They needed help. As their librarian, he could help.

I wanted to look closely at the librarians in a particular institution, someplace you could see change happening. What, I wondered, did the digital age look like at a brick-and-mortar library in transition—and not just any library, but the landmark New York Public Library at Forty-second Street and Fifth Avenue. It is a great American library, and one of the great libraries of the world. And it's changing faster than most, changing before our eyes.

I sat behind the library in Bryant Park on a winter's day and tried to keep its history in perspective as Gertrude Stein peered down from her marble perch and a bronze William Cullen Bryant entertained the pigeons. The ground it stands on is a palimpsest. This was once a potter's field full of cholera victims.

Then it was a reservoir. Then the reservoir was drained and for years, at the turn of the last century, it was a muddy construction site.

This day, the library was draped in canvas and plastic; a fifty-million-dollar cleaning and facelift had begun. Even the canvas and plastic looked chic; a temporary barricade was a white partition, painted charmingly with ivy. Tourists gathered inside and out, snapping photographs. The fall plantings had been lifted from their beds and an ice-skating rink laid in, so we could twirl if we liked in meaningless circles while contemplating the mysterious business of trying to adapt a nearly hundred-year-old library to the digital age.

What happens here ripples through multiple overlapping worlds—the universe of scholars, past, present, and future; the population of New York; the tourist industry, the publishing business, big philanthropy, and the writer who can't find a book. And, naturally, what happens in this library happens to its librarians. In the first decade of the twenty-first century, at the intersection of rapid change and financial meltdown, some of its librarians carve out a niche, some get iced out, and some help plan the future of the library and how we use it. You could sit in the park, watching the seasons change, and feel that civilization would be fine, if only the people in charge could get the mix right.

I came across a wonderful quote in Nicholas A. Basbanes's book about books, *Patience and Fortitude*, named for the stone lions that guard this library. Attributed to John Willis Clark, an antiquarian book expert who died early in the twentieth century, the quote reads: "a library may be described as a gigantic mincing-machine into which the labours of the past are flung, to be turned out again in a slightly altered form as the literature of the present." Books are sausages made by writers.

"The library does outreach for kindergartners, Spanish-speaking patrons, job-seekers. Why not this important constituency?" Smith said. Libraries inhaled writers and exhaled their work—not just the books they wrote, but their readings and programs; and their papers and manuscripts filled the archives. They were a living part of this living organism. The NYPL honored famous writers every year at its $1,500-a-head gala, but Smith thought it should also honor its writing stiffs and working joes, those who over the years took the resources of the library and turned them into "the literature of the present." After months of lobbying, he got the administration's blessings to throw a holiday party for authors who "used the collections"—writers who had borrowed a desk in one of the writers' rooms, or had showed up looking for material and happened to mention they were writers, or who came in and scribbled under one of those brass lamps. He intended the party as a gracious message from the library: *Think of this place as a home for you, your books, your legacy.*

I met him in the center of the food court in Grand Central, at a table laminated with suburban train tickets and schedules and covered with crumbs. Smith opened his briefcase and plucked out the invitation list and a stack of copied invitations to "An NYPL Holiday Season Reception Honoring Authors Using the Collections," guest-hosted by Roy Blount, Jr. A picture of the library's sculpted lions was faintly visible in the background, almost like a watermark. Guests were invited to come in "Writing Attire" and feel free to "BYOBook," that is, bring a copy of one of their own books to display at the party.

In Smith's dream, the head of NYPL's research libraries, David Ferriero, would stand up at the celebration—an annual event, possibly?—and announce the creation of an Office for Writers' Services, which would recognize the library's special relationship with its neediest, and most productive, patrons.

Smith described his campaign to get approval and funds from multiple departments in the library administration in boxing terms: "I've been bounced around, I got roughed up a couple of times. I keep thinking I'm in the ring and no matter how tired I am, I have to keep going." The harrowing business of trying to reach out and celebrate his patrons! The music was arranged, a Cajun cellist Smith heard on the street and loved. Smith offered him $150, which he agreed to initially, but later decided wasn't enough. Smith told the guy the names of some of the writers who would be there. Didn't he get it? The librarian from Carnegie Hall was going to be there! Finally Smith told him, " 'Dude, show up and play, or don't show up and play.' "

Smith labored over his e-mails to writers, partly out of self-consciousness. He told me he had heard from Tony Kushner, the great playwright who wrote *Angels in America*, and

Nick Tosches, the music journalist. Impressed, his wife, Debbi Smith, an academic librarian at Adelphi University, said, "And to think, I married this quiet librarian!"

I ran my eyes down the guest list, full of familiar and not-so-familiar names. "Who's this?" I wondered. "Nina Burleigh—she just wrote a fantastic book about Napoleon's invasion of Egypt." Smith ran down the list, explaining the contribution each guest made to the culture: "Oh, she's writing a book about lighthouse keepers, but don't tell anyone. . . . He wrote a boxing book you've got to read. . . . She writes the funny librarian sketches for *Prairie Home Companion*; I'll send you some. . . . And that's Barbara, the librarian at the American Kennel Club."

Wait a minute. A dog librarian? "Oh yeah," he said, "she's got a beautiful library. I have to bring her an invitation. You want to come? It's, like, four blocks from here." I'd been avoiding getting a dog for twenty years. Surely I could avoid the dog librarian? And what was a dog librarian doing at the writers' party, anyway?

In the lull between the morning rush hour and the afternoon bustle, someone on Grand Central's cleanup crew began disinfecting tables. An ammonia wind drifted our way, driving us out of the food tunnel and out the doors of the train station. Somehow we found ourselves walking toward the American Kennel Club Library.

There are thousands of buildings lining the canyons of Manhattan, some more ornate than others, but I never saw one with a lobby floor like that at 260 Madison. Smith signed in with the guard and headed toward the elevator, but I lingered over the art beneath my feet: the two-dimensional globe in brass and Mediterranean blue, the Greek border. Decorating the hall upstairs, by the library, were eight display cases with little brass sculptures of dogs. Through the big glass double doors, a giant oil painting of a purebred something gazed prayerfully toward a beam of light. There was a guard or butler sitting at an ornate reception desk. Smith shambled past him and we headed left through more doors and into the library of an English hunting lodge—anyway, that was the effect, a sense of gleaming order and privilege.

Behind the greeting desk, on which lay an old-fashioned guest book, glass cases displayed massive loving cups, including an oversized one for Pekingese; behind it, a photo of the cup with a Pekingese nestling inside. Presiding over one of the long tables was a glass case containing the skeleton of a midsized dog, and in the winter light streaming in the window he seemed to be looking down his bony jaw at the sole patron, a gentleman studying an old book of pedigrees. The skeleton was not that of any old dog, but of Belgrave Joe, a celebrity dog that died in 1888. We were in a shrine to The Dog, the dog of literature, journalism, and art; the dog of history; its purebred expression; its idealized state. There was no evidence of any wet, muddy, smelly, or mangy mongrels.

New York is full of these gems, little libraries and archives that capture a slice of the past and, in a disorderly and even chaotic world, organize the knowledge and art of, say, Louis Armstrong, or botanical gardens, or pornography (the Museum of Sex owns a collection of pornography painstakingly cataloged over the years by a Library of Congress librarian). The New York Society Library, a subscription library nestled in an Upper East Side town house, has a sweeping staircase and a beautiful old room for its old card catalog ("The members would never let me give this away," its head librarian says). The fabulous Morgan Library and Museum, with its illuminated manuscripts and Rembrandt etchings, is three blocks down Madison. And . . . not complaining, but . . . here we were in the American Kennel Club Library.

The dog librarian was in her late fifties, with neatly cut graying hair and rimless glasses, a jeweled pin of a Scotty on her red boiled wool jacket. Barbara Kolb used to work in public relations for *Good Housekeeping* and Macy's, but she never felt she fit in. She would go off to find some information she needed, and find all this other stuff, too. "I was always getting sidetracked."

In thirteen years here, Kolb had organized the library, modernized its online catalog, and linked it to WorldCat, in between serving the information needs of the American Kennel Club and its magazine and stray members of the general public who wander in and ask about labradoodles or the Westminster Dog Show. Her kingdom comprises eighteen thousand volumes, more or less, some of them rare and irreplaceable, in seventeen languages—two thousand years of writing about dogs, including the only complete set of *English Kennel Club* magazine in the United States. Other libraries can be ruthless when it comes to their space, but "what's a great policy in one library can be a horrible policy in another. People say, 'Let's weed the stacks!' For the public library, maybe, but not for a research library." Recently, Kolb had been collecting old children's literature about dogs. "I've found some very good and rare dog books on eBay," she said. "I keep my mouth shut and very quietly buy books for the library." She showed me *The Dog's Dinner Party*, the old tale of an eighteenth-century eccentric, an earl who habitually dined with his twelve dogs, assigning them each a footman who served them on silver plates. "You can get some bargains on eBay!"

I could live here, I thought. I could study dogs and help this lovely dog librarian . . . "Come back anytime," she said as I tore myself away, "though we're crazy the week of the dog show!"

The reception for writers was held the first night of Hanukkah, a conflict caught too late to change. The writer Esmeralda Santiago and I got all dolled up in satin and velvet, swishy skirts and heeled boots. Ascending the marble steps, I felt dressed for the library's grandeur for the first time.

We found David Smith in the Catalog Room, exhausted. He'd gone to an author's book party the previous night in Queens, caught a late train home, and slept for all of three or four hours. "Have a seat, have a seat," he said, dislodging some papers so we could crowd in. "I'm a wreck," Smith kept saying. And then: "Have you seen Roy Blount? He said he was coming to do some research around three. You don't have his cell number, do you?"

Santiago and I wanted to help, so we went looking for the humorist and president of the Authors Guild. Strolling in our fancy clothes like fine Victorian ladies along the boulevard, we cruised the long aisle of the Rose Reading Room, our heels echoing on the terrazzo floors; then it was downstairs through the periodicals section, and even into the microforms room, where a row of microfilm machines lined the far wall. I looked around that corner, though it occurred to me that if Blount was there, he didn't want to be found, and what would I say, anyway? "The librarian got nervous, so I'm stalking you?" We gave up and meandered back upstairs, where we saw Smith directing one of his colleagues in the wheeling of a book cart. "There are the books for the party," Santiago said, the books written by the party guests. We fell in behind the two librarians, giving them an entourage, and a parade.

The Trustees Room was elegant with tapestries and marble fixtures, the great chandelier in the middle of the room twisted with greenery, the brocade drapes framing big windows. Past the winter tree branches, the lights and horns of a traffic jam added to the festivities. It was holiday season, we were in a place of beauty and tradition; we had looked up from our dusty tomes and smudged computer screens and been transformed from solitary drudges into a community of honored guests. Smith could have served us Cheez Whiz.

He moved energetically from table to musician to bar, and at last Blount arrived as the room began to fill and buzz. The center of attention wasn't the bar or the buffet of shrimp and cheese and cookies, but the table of books by the writers who worked in the library; it was surrounded by partygoers turning the pages of wonderful books you might never have heard of: *The Violin Maker*; *Corner Men*; *First into Nagasaki*; *Lucky Girls*; *The History of the Snowman*; and in pride of place in the center, a special nod to two authors who had died the past year but had also worked here: *On God,* by Norman Mailer, and *The Coldest Winter: America and the Korean War*, by David Halberstam, both published posthumously.

The party had already spilled out into the hall when Smith's boss, David Ferriero, raised a toast to "the first annual writers' celebration, a long overdue tribute to your contributions to literature and scholarship," and to David Smith, who had done such a fine job connecting authors with information and whose support had made such a difference to "the creative voices of the city." Smith, proud and blushing, read his remarks to more cheers from his patrons, the writers, and their enablers, the librarians.

It was a beautiful moment, not to be spoiled by a looming future: there would be no Office of Writers' Services, and no funds, either, for a second or third annual reception for writers. But even if we could have seen that coming, and seen that Smith himself would be offered a retirement package and leave early in the summer of 2009, it wouldn't have spoiled the mood.

It was Blount's turn to speak. He took the microphone and told a shaggy-dog story about lining up in the marble hall with a bunch of honored authors for the NYPL gala one year, waiting to be introduced into a great glittering room full of socialites and fancy people, and being shushed—though "you kind of hate to be shushed if you are a Literary Lion." The introductions had not apparently been synced with the actual entrances, and as Blount stood poised to go through the doors, he heard Barbara Walters announcing "A humorist . . . a novelist . . . and incidentally a very good cook," and it caused him some consternation. Was he, perhaps without even knowing it, a good cook? "I have done things late at night that I don't remember, and as a writer, you want to remember . . ." At any rate, with that introduction, he jogged into the great Rose Reading Room, transformed into the scene of a gala, only to find everybody cheering for . . . Nora Ephron.

It was the ideal story to tell on this occasion. Magazines and newspapers got skinnier every week; bookstores and publishers were increasingly platforms for brands; on the Web, writers were "content providers." Sometimes, it felt like writers were on their way to becoming the telegraph operators of the twenty-first century. But here in this room, on this night, there were still people who could tell—and celebrate—the difference between Roy Blount, Jr., and Nora Ephron.

Blount had only one burning question before he let the gratified crowd return to its revels: "Will the librarian for the American Kennel Club please identify herself? The novelist Cathleen Schine is dying to meet you."

The first librarian hired to run the New York Public, Dr. John Shaw Billings, designed the layout of the building himself in the late nineteenth century, and it was tricky getting an architectural firm to implement it—McKim, Mead & White, for instance, didn't care to execute someone else's plan, particularly if that someone was not an architect, but a librarian. But this librarian knew what he was doing—the stacks were closed, hidden away from the public, yet integrated into the structure of the building. The books gave the illusion of supporting the main reading room, arranged as they were on iron shelves custom-carved by Carrère and Hastings, the architectural firm that had agreed to take direction from Billings, and ended up making its reputation with this project. The reading room was housed on the third floor in a tremendous vaultlike space, insulated from the noise and bustle of midtown Manhattan and topped by the kind of ceiling you'd see in an Italian villa, all clouds and sky painted a deep powdery blue. Down the length of the room—two football fields long, as everyone loves to say—stretched heavy custom-made tables, lit by brass lamps that can be purchased in the gift shop downstairs for $375. Many of the tables now hold computers, free for public use; anyone can walk in and check e-mail. And anyone can get a card and order up any of the precious holdings of the vast research library, to read and examine on the premises. The halls are clogged with tourists; homeless guys mingle with writers at the tables; but unlike the branch libraries, there's a lovely old-fashioned hush in here. It's a research library.

People call this building the New York Public Library, but that's misleading. The New York Public Library is a system of eighty-nine libraries, most of them considerably less glamorous than this one. When I first started haunting the place, it was called the Humanities and Social Sciences Library—but under any name it attracts scholars from around the world, as do the three other jewels of the system: the Performing Arts Library at Lincoln Center; the Schomburg Center for Research in Black Culture, in Harlem; and the Science, Industry, and Business Library. The one guarded by lions is the most famous of all, and durable in a way that few monuments to the written word seem to be these days. Even if they wanted to, the NYPL librarians could never digitize everything there in our lifetime. We'll always need a place for the early Gutenberg Bibles, the Declaration of Independence (handwritten by Jefferson), and the *yizkor* memorial books, all that's left of various Jewish communities erased over the years, from the First Crusade in the eleventh century to the Holocaust. We'll always need printed books that don't mutate the way digital books do; we'll always need places to display books, auditoriums for book talks, circles for story time; we'll always need brick-and-mortar libraries. But another library, the ninetieth in the system, is growing explosively in cyberspace.

If my laptop carried only one Web address, NYPL.org, I could be entertained for months by its Digital Collections, with some new chunk of knowledge or new delivery system appearing every time I check—the books the library ships out to

Google for digitization, scanned now and accessible; lectures and readings, linked through iTunes; NYPL's librarian blogs. It's alive!

Joshua Greenberg, tall, young, and crowned with a dark mop of curls, has the coolest job in the world. No wonder he radiates joy. A few years ago, the NYPL invested many resources devising a way to digitally photograph, catalog, and upload thousands of images to its website; then it looked around and went, *Now what?* Josh Greenberg's job was to figure out *what*. He was hired at the age of thirty, three years out of a Ph.D. program, and given the title director of digital strategy and scholarship. "I'm trained as an historian, but I'm a weird intellectual mongrel. I come out of a discipline called Science and Technology Studies," he said. Greenberg's thesis and the subject of his first book was the history of video stores. He inherited the digital library program, "which had already digitized something like six hundred thousand items. It was this amazing resource, but it wasn't integrated with the rest of the library. There wasn't a central policy about what went in and why."

Well, so what, you might say. What's the difference between 600,000 fabulous digital pictures of things chosen somewhat haphazardly, and the same number of equally fabulous things that reflected a policy and design? It's the difference between a storehouse of books and a library; a bunch of old stuff about baseball and the Baseball Hall of Fame; walls full of impressionist art and the Musée d'Orsay. It's why a library needs specialists in acquisitions, people who know enough about a field to stock a collection that illuminates and explains it.

Greenberg had spent his three postdoctorate years working with the Center for History and New Media at George Mason University, essentially structuring digital information, and had learned the value of integrating it with the rest of the library and, most important, with the library's users.

He proceeded by starting something he called the Digital Experience Group. The name pleased him, because it sounds like a sixties happening. "It ultimately says that we're not concerned with digital technology for its own sake. We're not concerned with the collections for their own sake. We're concerned with people's experience. There are certain tools like 'user experience design' or 'user analysis' that have been integral to the way that the dot-com world works and are just starting to make their way into the library world. This turn toward the user is huge in libraries right now."

There were fifteen people in his Digital Experience Group; about half of them had come from I-schools, great library schools that had reconfigured themselves as "information schools." Everyone on his staff had librarian values, loads of technical training, and an eagerness to think broadly and creatively about the role of a library in the digital and cultural landscape. While other departments in the library system are losing librarians through attrition, Greenberg was still hiring (he had planned to hire ten more, but the economic crisis later that year limited him to three).

His digital group started with the basics. When people click NYPL.org, what do they find? Libraries took it for granted that you came onto a home page and jumped from there to the catalog or the databases, but Greenberg said, "In the era of Google and Yahoo!, that's not good enough."

He created a webpage he called the Digital Labs, where his staff members could post their thoughts and findings and pose questions, and he opened it up, not just to other library employees, but to anyone out there who wanted to be part of the conversation. It's a fascinating glimpse into the cyber back room of the library, accessible to all who visit the website NYPL.org, and welcoming to anyone with any level of expertise. "Hey, are you a user? Then your input is invaluable!" it says in numerous ways. It felt like Romper Room, with a bunch of postgrads cooking up a neat show with neat stuff from the vaults of history. Its banner was a metaphysical drawing of a head with a mapped skull and circles going into it and coming out restructured, under the legend "The Process Behind the Product."

"We wanted to establish a sense that we're under construction, possibly in perpetuity," Greenberg said. "As the ground keeps shifting, we've got to keep shifting with it." He cited Google's always-under-construction policy with approval. "They make a commitment to their users that, 'Hey, here's this thing; it pretty much works. If it breaks occasionally, we're sorry. It's because we're making it better.' And that's the posture that the library needs to take. There are certain core things like the catalog that need to work. But beyond that, there's no way we're going to get in the game and stay where users expect if we don't always reach for more."

He mentioned one of the contributors to the Digital Labs, a library consultant who did a study of how young people live on the Internet and how they do their homework. "We came to the conclusion that if we just built a traditional website, it's more or less throwing money away. We need to take our services into the places the kids already are." What they were designing then was a widget, a little box that students could park on their desktop or Facebook page, that they could click to bring them directly to what they needed at the library.

In the course of reintegrating the digital library, Greenberg had roped in librarians to contribute to an NYPL blog. The reference librarian with an interest in the culinary arts wrote about menus and recipes. The map librarian blogged about how to get the most out of Google Earth and aerial photos of New York City from 1924. Someone from adult outreach explained how to pronounce *Wii*, and told us where we could learn to play such a thing (the library, for one). Digital wasn't something that only the people in the digital group did.

Greenberg was fostering active librarians for the mash-up generation, for potential patrons who could take the library's resources and create something new with them. "Before, everybody wasn't publishing books. Everybody wasn't creating movies," he said. The trend to create and share, especially on the Web, "is much more visible now. And we have to figure out—what's the role of the librarian supporting that?"

Librarians weren't necessarily ready to rethink the library for the new zeitgeist, he felt; and libraries aren't especially structured to encourage creativity in their staffs. But why should they be different from any other institutions these days? Look at the 2008 election, "where the grassroots has taken on such importance. There's this real tension," he said—between the old, hierarchical institutions and the freewheeling cacophony of individual voices. "All this other stuff is happening that resonates with a more active role for librarians. It's messy," he said, cheerfully.

Like most American libraries, the NYPL has seen hard times. During the fiscal crisis of the mid-1970s, when New York City went bankrupt, an event memorialized by the *Daily News* headline FORD TO CITY: DROP DEAD, the libraries starved. The library on Fifth Avenue was dirty. Its beautiful Celeste Bartos Forum, now a jewel of a performance center, was being used as a warehouse for old furniture. Masonite walls divided up the exhibition area, and the lightbulbs had burned out. Vartan Gregorian, the college president who took on the job of its rejuvenation in 1981, described the back of the building that faced Bryant Park as "New York's longest urinal."

Gregorian turned the library from a beggar into a queen during his eight-year tenure by courting benefactors, lobbying the city, and articulating over and over again that the library was not a charity but a philanthropy, not a luxury we could do without, but worthy of being lavished with funds, and as valuable to the cultural life of this city as the Metropolitan Museum or Lincoln Center. He took a place that served jug wine in plastic cups to its donors and turned it into a place that threw galas to rival the Met's in opulence.

And the library is run like a philanthropy, quietly, by a board of trustees and a few high-powered, highly paid administrators. Paul LeClerc, the president and CEO, earns a CEO-style salary (almost $800,000 in 2007), and David Ferriero does nicely with half that. Its regular librarians, however, aren't paid so handsomely; in fact, the NYPL ranked twenty-fifth out of twenty-five libraries in a 2005 *American Libraries* survey, with starting salaries then of less than $36,000 a year—and that in the most expensive city in the country.

The website refers to the tangle of civic and philanthropic funds that finance the system as a "still evolving private-public partnership." It's called the New York *Public* Library, and the city of New York owns the building on Fifth Avenue and many of the circulating libraries, and pays for the administration of the circulating libraries and their staffs. The research collections and most of the research staff are the bailiwick of a non-profit foundation, the New York Public Library Astor Lenox and Tilden Foundations. Its tax returns are public, but you won't find the minutes of the board meetings online. Debate about the future of the library happens behind closed doors. The administration and the board don't have to slow down for contentious New York constituency groups, and almost everything they do comes as a surprise to the patrons, like the news that the beloved Donnell Library—a branch with a devoted community of patrons and unique collections of books in world languages and films—would be dismantled, sold, then turned into a much smaller library beneath a luxury hotel; or the day everyone learned that the world-renowned research library on Fifth Avenue was changing its name and, oh, by the way, its identity.

News of Eliot Spitzer's scandal, his dalliance with a four-thousand-dollar prostitute, and speculation about his resignation as governor of New York dwarfed the other news of March 11, 2008: the bombing in Baghdad that killed five U.S. soldiers; the downward-spiraling economy, as seen through the lens of the buyout firm, the Blackstone Group, and the billions draining out of its CEO Stephen A. Schwarzman's pockets; and at the bottom of the front page, another story about Schwarzman: FOR $100 MILLION, A LIBRARY CARD AND PERHAPS HIS NAME IN STONE. Schwarzman was giving the biggest gift in its history to the New York Public Library, kick-starting a billion-dollar renovation of the Fifth Avenue building and the creation of two new hub libraries. The donation was so spectacular—"among the largest to any cultural institution in the city's history"—that the library would be renamed the Stephen A. Schwarzman Building in his honor.

But naming the library after Schwarzman was the gossipy part of the story, the $100 million, a diamond flashing in our eyes, the fur coat wrapped around the real news: the research stacks were being shifted out of the building at Forty-second and Fifth and into underground storage so a circulating library could be squeezed in. "The average user of our branch libraries wasn't coming to Forty-second Street," a library spokesman said. "This new plan was the further democratization of that building." A million annual visitors would be turning into four million. President LeClerc named the constituencies he wanted to see coming through the doors: "teenagers working on term papers, graduate students writing theses, rare book aficionados searching out volumes, and children flocking to story hour."

Phrases like "children flocking to story hour" go down like hot chocolate any day. But when a powerful politician falls, nobody's talking about story time or the future of libraries. You might not notice that a world-class research library had just agreed to make room for children, teenagers, and DVDs; and unless you were a writer you might not notice that writers hadn't made the list of patrons the library was eager to see coming through the door.

David Ferriero, a distinguished-looking gentleman with gray temples, strolled the marble halls, swinging his glasses. The distinctions between the research libraries and the circulating libraries were melting on his watch, and months after the library announced its new plans, Ferriero had gone from directing the four research libraries to directing *all* of the libraries.

Ferriero had modernized Duke University's libraries before he came to NYPL in 2004. I admired him for taking on the warehouse full of newspapers that the writer Nicholson Baker accumulated after Baker learned of the trashing and discarding of the irreplaceable newspapers by the British Library, the Library of Congress, and others. Baker's nonfiction screed *Double Fold: Libraries and the Assault on Paper* was rough on librarians, but it's impossible to read it without wondering how anyone, especially someone educated and committed to the preservation and dissemination of knowledge, could justify destroying something as precious as the last complete run of an illustrated newspaper more than a century old.

Ferriero saved Baker from a self-imposed sentence tending a climate-controlled warehouse full of old, rare newspapers and took in the whole lot for Duke University's libraries, where they now rest in perpetuity. For that act alone, he's a capable steward of the treasures of the past.

But, like library administrators everywhere, he is trying to balance the need to preserve the past with the pressure to speed up technological expansion, all on a shrinking budget. At the NYPL, Ferriero has earned a reputation for his digital savvy. He hired Greenberg, the digital guru. Under his and Paul LeClerc's direction, NYPL was one of the first libraries to sign up for the Google Books Digitization Project, firmly committing the library's older, out-of-copyright books while the project was still controversial. Ferriero weaned the library off an antique cataloging system devised a hundred years ago by Billings, the original head librarian (it now catalogs its holdings using the Library of Congress classification system, the academic alternative to the Dewey Decimal System); and he has been at the front of the historic consolidation of the libraries. Not only was he now in charge of circulating as well as research libraries, he was leading the effort to combine their separated catalogs, though this transition turned out to be nearly as harrowing as Westchester County's catalog migration. A *New York Times* story in the summer of 2009 reported a scene remarkably similar to the one in Westchester two years earlier, when technology glitches frayed the nerves of both patrons and librarians.

The first casualties of the planned consolidation were not announced anywhere else. The signs were Scotch-taped to the doors of the two reading rooms of the Asian and Middle Eastern Division: the Newspaper & Microform Reading Room and the exquisite Shoichi Noma Reading Room: AS OF SEPTEMBER 2, 2008, THE ASIAN AND MIDDLE EASTERN READING ROOMS ARE PERMANENTLY CLOSED.

The sheets instructed patrons to visit the reference desk or the Rare Books Reading Room if they wanted access to the collection. A similar sign was taped to the door across the hall, the reading room of the Baltic and Slavic collection, which holds, among other items, the papers of the czars, sold by a strapped Soviet Union.

The former head of the Asian and Middle Eastern Division worked just down the hall from the shuttered reading rooms, in an office carved out of the past; it felt like a secret room tucked under the eaves, too much furniture, wooden cabinets and tables piled high with unopened mail. An industrial-sized air conditioner loomed menacingly over the doorway; a few moments after it rumbled into action, its runoff could be heard draining behind one of the bookcases. The room, I was told, used to be a shower for porters in the library's early days.

Disorder was not John Lundquist's natural state. He was tall and old-school, with a somewhat mournful bearing, a haircut you might have seen in the 1920s, parted in the middle, a long layer on top, cut close below, round tortoiseshell glasses, a black suit with black textured tie—a refined presence, as if he'd been polished at Oxford, or just come from tea with T. S. Eliot. The mess was evidence of one of the sacrifices the research library was making in order to absorb the circulating library across the street. "Our division has been dissolved. Our reading rooms have been closed. Our librarians have been reassigned. I'm no longer the head of the division; I'm now a curator. In theory we continue as collections, the Asian and the Baltic, but I'm highly skeptical. Our material is available if scholars want it—it's upstairs on the third floor, and the valuable items are in a locked cage that can be accessed through the Rare Books Reading Room. But as a result of the merger between research and the branch libraries, we have been downsized. The whole library has been drastically downsized.

"Our staff of twenty-two had been approximately halved in this last phase. The retirees are not replaced. That is ongoing. When the Arabic-language cataloger retires, we will be without an Arabic-language librarian. We've already lost Persian, Korean, and a number of the languages of India. I don't see them being replaced, ever."

His staff has been reassigned to cataloging, not to reference, where they might be able to help the regular staff with the sort of technical, scholarly foreign-language requests that are now being directed there. "There has been nothing about this in the press, no. Obviously the library doesn't want any publicity. In the view of senior management, this change is, in fact, an improvement. It's almost Orwellian. They foresee many thousands more people in the building, and that, to them, is a worthy goal. There is a perception that libraries are archaic, dead, outdated, and that everything is now on the Internet, in digital form. We are old, stooped-over people doing old, stooped-over things. They want to lighten things up, they want the library to be active and hip, they want to put in a cafeteria and schedule entertainments—they want us to join the modern age.

"I gave a talk about my new book across the street at the Mid-Manhattan branch. That place is utter chaos. And it will all come here—the noise, the teenage programs, the circulating DVDs."

Lundquist's book, *The Temple of Jerusalem: Past, Present, and Future,* is a scholarly work about a temple from the age of King Solomon, which doesn't survive; not even a fragment of a ruin survives. Lundquist reconstructs it based on eyewitness accounts, scripture, and historic records, using an impressive breadth of references, from the Hebrew Bible to the Coptic Gnostic texts of Nag Hammadi, to the writings of medieval Jewish, Christian, and Islamic pilgrims.

The people who took his scholarly division away lavishly celebrated the publication of his scholarly book. "Paul LeClerc and David Ferriero gave me an extraordinary book party in September. Many, many library staff members came, my friends and family—I have six children—were there. Really, it was very generous of them, and I don't know that such a gesture has ever been made to a librarian here before." So September was a good month and a bad month.

The director with no one to direct had turned into a curator with too many things to curate. The odd part of this downsizing was that, although his reading room had been taken and his staff dispersed, his acquisitions budget had increased. New books, magazines, photographs, and art from Asia and the Middle East continued to pour through the door, but his former staff librarians "all have different supervisors now. We do continue to collaborate on acquisitions, but we have to find the time to do that work." It led to messes like this room. He said he was frequently interrupted by the stream of librarians from Mid-Manhattan, the circulating branch across Fifth Avenue, who would soon be moving from a space that resembled a department store (and was, in fact, a former department store), into marble and gleaming wood, and who could barely conceal their excitement from Lundquist. The little jewel box, the Shoichi Noma Reading Room, was renovated in 1997 by the head of Kodansha, a Japanese publisher, who donated more than a million dollars in his father's memory to buff it up with cork floors edged in marble, an elaborate desk for the librarian, brass and wood steps to a balcony lined with books. The bequest was honored by the library at the gala, and Shoichi Noma's widow accepted the award. Someone in the administration was trying to compose a letter to let them know that their gift would no longer be used to host parts of the Asia and Middle East collection, and called Lundquist for help, but he didn't know what to say, either.

Why didn't he just leave? "If I left now, it would be a disaster. I have all this institutional knowledge, and this is a crucial transitional period. Things would disappear, be misplaced, get lost or dumped."

He showed me some of his treasures in the locked cages
of the stacks, late-nineteenth-century photographs of Mecca,
recently salvaged by the conservation lab in the basement and
"of great historic value and endless potential for scholars," he
said. "We have one of the greatest collections in the world of
what I call Orientalism, Western scholars and explorers dis-
covering Asia." Images of some of the books and scrolls can
be seen online in the collection's digital holdings. Lundquist
appreciates the work the digitization staff has done—"one of
the greatest achievements of this administration," he said.

The most exciting acquisition was a complete set of prints
from the hand-engraved woodblocks of the Tibetan monas-
tery of Dege: about eight hundred volumes, arriving by ship
over the course of three years. Among all the muted reds and
blacks and browns of the stacks were carts piled high with
these printings, bundled in bright-yellow flags with embroidered end flaps, gift-wrapped offerings from another culture.
The first shipment was in the process of being cataloged by
one part-time librarian and two volunteers from a Buddhist
library.

Lundquist opened one of the intricately folded yellow bun-
dles, brushed off the paper dust on the cover, sounded out the
letters, and explained that this volume was about a branch
of Buddhist philosophy. It was exotic, red ink in a code I
couldn't read, on textured paper, about three times as wide as
it was tall. Why was it wrapped so carefully, even ceremoni-
ally in that flag? Why were the edges of the book painted red?
These were signs of respect; the monks do not want the book

to be naked, so they clothe it with paint and fabric. "If we were Buddhists, we would touch the manuscript to our foreheads," he said, "like so, as a blessing," and the librarian lifted the manuscript and touched it to his head to demonstrate.

Outside his office, a lone man sat reading at one of the carved tables, opposite the two closed reading rooms. "This used to be a quite active corridor," Lundquist said. "It's a dead zone now. It is a main corridor that cuts through the center of the building and will be an obvious route for the public to get to the stacks, which are behind that door and which are going to be taken out and turned into a circulating library. I think we are just an accident of our geography. It's not so much that they don't want us. . . . [The Asia collection] is simply in a space that they require for other purposes."

The whole time Lundquist spoke, he looked at me steadily; his tone was flat and deadpan, punctuated occasionally by a wan smile. This is the way of the world now; if bombs were dropping, he'd estimate their distance and force. And within a year, he would no longer work here.

"I'm terribly sad about it," he said. "In due time no one will remember we existed. These rooms will be reoccupied, and all will be forgotten. I'm quite certain we will be forgotten."

The NYPL press officer received my request to sit in on a trustees' meeting with surprise and asked a number of questions. I mentioned that I had been the beneficiary of a key to one of the writers' rooms; that I had done programs for the library; that I had already talked to a dozen or more librarians—"You interviewed librarians?" he said, alarmed. Didn't he get requests like that all the time? What about the *New York Times*? No, the press doesn't come. So how do they know when something is happening? He sends them press releases.

This is surprising for an institution that relies on public funds as much as this one, but the press is shrinking, and so is press coverage. Within twenty-four hours of asking, however, I had permission to attend the February 11, 2009, trustees' meeting, to be held at the Schomburg Center for Research in Black Culture. By then, almost a year had passed since the announcement of the ambitious remaking of the research library, and the economy had tanked. Now what? Where would the librarians and the trustees with the high-beam flashlights strapped to their foreheads take us next?

The Schomburg Center in Harlem is a lovely brick building three stories high, a fraction of the size of its sister library at Forty-second and Fifth. I headed downstairs to the research and reading rooms, clean and modern, with views of a little brick courtyard with ivy-covered walls. The elevator opened onto a sweeping reference desk, where a sharp-eyed librarian named Sharon Jarvis snagged me.

It's hard to say who interviewed whom. "I've been spending time at the main library," I began and she smiled. "We don't call it the *main library* here. Have you been to the Bronx Hub?" She was referring to a modern and successful community library, open till nine at night, hopping with patrons, and circulating material like mad; this was the model the trustees wanted to replicate in two other locations. I confessed I hadn't been yet. Jarvis worked there on Sundays sometimes, and she recommended it. Jarvis tilted her head—she was in her fifties, I'd guess, with pulled-back braids and a broad pretty face; she had two master's degrees, including her library degree, and this was her third career—and extracted my résumé before giving me a tour of the holdings from her computer, skipping around the archives and showing me what was possible to look at, the papers of the singer Mabel Mercer, for instance, or some, but only some, of the papers of Malcolm X (his heirs had left restrictions).

I settled in at one of the slate tables rimmed with pale wood and started writing, but before I got very far, Jarvis came over and dropped a volume on my desk: *The Handbook of Black Librarianship*. "I don't know whether this would interest you," she began. It certainly did. Its coeditor E. J. Josey, I learned, had spoken out in 1964 against ALA officers and staff for attending, on the ALA's dime, the meetings of the four state library associations that still practiced segregation. Twenty years later, Josey became the second African-American president of the ALA. He was a visionary, too, as his writing showed. "Information justice is a human rights issue; the public library must remain 'the people's university' . . . and librarians can get involved and shape the future or they can sit back and watch the changes." Like a great reference librarian, Jarvis had given me what I didn't know I needed, perspective on a profession that, even now, was only 5 percent black and 3 percent Latino. (Why? There is so much education required, and so little pay and prestige for the work.) A few months later, I read Josey's obituaries when he died at the age of eighty-five.

I followed a couple of well-heeled gentlemen into the elevator to the trustees' meeting, in a big, modern, asymmetrical room. Long tables arranged in a rectangle took up almost the whole space, with places for nearly forty board members, all dressed up, suits everywhere, and the occasional strand of pearls. "You'll sit over here," I was told, on one of two wings where folding chairs had been set. "With the press?" I said. "There's no press," my guide said. I knew that; I was just needling her. In fact, I was sitting with staffers, aides, the new professional lobbyist who was being introduced that evening. It was like a Senate hearing. I recognized almost every nameplate within eyesight, from Catherine Marron (the chairman) and Princess Firyal (of the Lionel Pincus and Princess Firyal Map Division at the not-main library), to the writer and philanthropist Barbara Goldsmith, to Calvin Trillin, to businessmen like James Tisch and Edgar Wachenheim and Joshua Steiner.

The meeting ran like an Acela, on high-speed tracks with minimal interruption (only one latecomer; only one board member slipped out early; only one brief trill of a cell) and little spontaneous discussion. The economy was bad, endowment was down, drops in city and state funds and donations were coming—but the NYPL would move forward, with the help of the captains of industry on its board. There were already savings initiatives in place, including a plan not to fill sixty-five vacant librarian positions (farewell, Persian-language librarian; goodbye, Baltic specialists).

Everyone spoke rapidly, so as not to waste time; the whole

meeting took seventy-five minutes. Statistics informed it all, a result of a strategic plan that had galvanized the chairman and the CEO and president, and made them determined to find out what the people of the city wanted in their libraries. The statistics, *the metrics*, the proof in the pudding: that fall, physical visits to the library had increased by 13 percent. Visits to the research centers had increased by a whopping 27 percent. Circulation at the branch libraries was up 18 percent. Curiously, materials usage in the research libraries was down by more than a quarter, maybe because wifi was now available in the entire reading room at Fifth Avenue and people were coming in just to check their e-mail.

The board was invited to help draft an up-to-date mission statement. They would meet in small groups over the next few weeks and help set their priorities. So far, these were their goals: to inspire life-long learning; to empower our communities; to bring together New York's diverse population to spark creativity and strengthen our cities.

These were wonderful goals—but if you were sitting in a world-class research library with a Wordsworth collection so good that British scholars had to come use it, and you knew Caribbean writers who cited its holdings of letters from Columbus to Luis de Santangel, Keeper of Accounts of Aragon, those goals seemed local, parochial, not big enough.

John Lundquist had put a beautiful volume from the Asian and Middle Eastern collection in my hand: Quentin Roosevelt II's dissertation on the Nashi (now called Naxi, or Nakhi) people, an ethnic group from the Himalayas with its own religion and language related to Tibetan. Who will use this book? A scholar of Chinese from Germany? A biographer of Quentin Roosevelt not yet born? Neither of these hypothetical people can be surveyed. The people who use research collections are unknown until they show up. If metrics measure worth, a research library might seem pointless; its collections are rarefied by definition.

Nicholas Basbanes tells a story about his search for a particular edition of *A Descriptive Catalogue of the Pepys Library*, not the 1829 or the 1978 editions—only the 1914 edition had the information he needed. He finally found its three volumes, untouched, in the basement of the Boston Athenaeum research library. "You wonder who they bought these books for, anyway," he said to the librarian. "We got them for *you*, Mr. Basbanes," he was told.

The hard choices are being made. The material, or much of it, is still there. But the librarians who understand it and can help people find and use some of those treasures are a disappearing breed.

The news about the architect who would spearhead the renovation of the Fifth Avenue library and pull it all together appeared seven months after the grand plan had been announced: Sir Norman Foster had the job. "NYPL's new architect announced . . . we're getting a big glass dome!! Seriously, though, very exciting," read the Twitter later that day from Josh Greenberg. Foster, who specializes in dramatic modern additions to historic buildings, had designed the British Museum's spectacular modern glass casing around the historic relic of a reading room from the British Library. He had done something similar for the Smithsonian in Washington, covering its stately nineteenth-century courtyard with an undulating glass roof.

To Jessica Pigza, reference librarian, the decisions of the trustees and the administration were a no-brainer: "It's great." She pointed out that there had been a circulating library in the Fifth Avenue building until 1970, when the Mid-Manhattan branch was created, so in her view things were coming full circle. People came to the library all the time wondering where the children's room was, or why they couldn't check out books, she said. It got tiresome explaining that it was a research library and everything had to stay on-site. She'd be happy when she could tell them otherwise. As for the library's choice of an architect, Sir Norman Foster was her favorite.

Pigza was in her thirties, one of the original members of the librarian social group, Desk Set. It was probably her fetching cat's-eye glasses that defined the new-wave librarians—she was pictured wearing them in the much-discussed article in the *New York Times*. The day we talked she was also in a beautiful turquoise dress that she'd made herself, with big antique buttons; she was "crafty," and described herself as an "enthusiast of books and other objects made by hand." Like the other reference librarians at the NYPL, she worked the desk for three or four hours a day and spent the rest of her time on projects, some of her own devising. "You can carve out your own niche here," she said with pride. Because she was interested in rare books, special collections, and the handmade arts, she taught occasional free classes for craft artists who want to use the library's resources for inspiration. She also wrote a blog for NYPL "about all this crazy stuff I find, like vintage knitting patterns." One day she came across the subject heading *soap sculpture* in the catalog and had to investigate. She posted a story about the craze for soap sculpture in the 1920s, when Procter & Gamble promoted it with contests and cash prizes. "Instead of just enjoying it and telling my husband about it when I get home, it lives on the Web now, where other people can find it." Every time I see Pigza or read her blog, I learn something new: Voltaire loved handcrafts, say, or the prisoners at San Quentin used to knit for the troops during World War I.

Like Pigza, Amy Azzarito had an interest in design; in addition to her library degree, she had a master's in the history of decorative arts and design. Josh Greenberg hired Azzarito as a digital producer in the spring of 2008, with the mission to get "the voices of the library and the librarians out onto the Web." Azzarito had worked at the library in various jobs, including designing classes for the public. "Instead of 'How to Use the Online Databases,' we offered classes like 'Cookery 101.' . . . We would talk about how to use the catalog or online database, but in the context of a subject."

For centuries, writers and scholars had been mashing up the contents of libraries and archives to create something new, taking correspondence and journals and turning them into biographies, pulling strands and pieces of others' arguments into a treatise of their own. But wouldn't it be interesting, the librarians thought—and, frankly, more fun—if artists mined the library the way writers did? Azzarito and Pigza plundered the NYPL collections for items they thought would inspire visual artists. Then they created a video series, tracking five young artists from their visits to the NYPL to their studios to their final art projects. They posted the results on the NYPL website and YouTube.

In the first episode, we met the artists, all of whom were young and lived in Brooklyn (no doubt next door to young librarians). There was a glassblower and four other artists working in a variety of media, porcelain jewelry, prints, wallpaper, and a self-described "maker" ("I just make things"). One of the artists admitted: "The library is a little intimidating. You don't want to bust through the doors and hunt down a librarian and say, 'I'm looking for a picture of a hydrangea!'"

In the second episode, the artists braved the library and met the charming Pigza—"I'm your librarian today!"—who spread a table for each with volumes of folding paper masks and fabric samples; old maps of Brooklyn and antique postcards; books on ghosts, terrariums, and WWII vintage navy uniforms. Anticipation continued to build in the third episode, in which the artists were seen working on their inspired art. After the third video was posted on the Web, the production team decided to give the fourth and final episode a ceremonial debut.

The RSVPs came rolling in via e-mail, from J. Crew and Ann Taylor and all sorts of independent design shops and blogs, artists and students—so many that the Trustees Room, the party's scheduled venue, was deemed too small. Instead, the display cases, the bar, the round table full of donated cupcakes (official snack of young librarians), and an information table stocked with brochures about the collections were all moved to the grand Celeste Bartos Forum. On a frigid night, they came, four hundred strong, to celebrate the debut of art inspired by the library.

David Ferriero and I were the oldest people in the room. "Do you believe this?" he said with obvious delight, as someone wheeled a stroller in, and arty young people in hand-knitted scarves clustered around the displays. Josh Greenberg beamed over the crowd. Jessica Pigza introduced me to the artist Julia Rothman, who had grabbed the book on navy uniforms and turned it into vintage-looking wallpaper, Sergeant Pepper–esque rows of uniformed men linked by loops of rope; she would give the whole venture a motto when she said: "I didn't know there was so much in there, waiting for us."

The art was displayed in the center of the room and the artists circulated through the party, but the video, the moving picture of the experience, was the point of the evening, the flickering happening that would capture the narrative of discovery and the spark of creation—simply because it was a video, an enveloping experience you could have in a group, in the dark, an event.

What was my problem? Though I loved the wired world, the new-wave librarians, the avatars and activists, I turned into a dinosaur in that library. I couldn't help it; I was an old-fashioned writer who loved the ancient books summoned via pneumatic tubes, the archives, the quiet. I had found something rare there: an inexhaustible wonder. The digital library hovering over it made the whole place only more wonderful and rich. But my heart had sunk the first time I went in the space that used to hold the *yizkor* memorial books and saw a phalanx of cheerful librarians welcome a toddler, the first or second child-patron through the door. Maybe this was just a New York story after all: I had laid claim to a little piece of the island, and I didn't want to give it up.

But I couldn't deny that there was something happening in the room of artists that thrilled me. I turned with the others toward the screen. A creative collaboration between librarians and patrons—isn't that a wonder, too? As the lights went down, those closest to the screen sank to the floor, and then the whole crowd behind them sank, too, a wave of hundreds of young people dropping to the floor and tilting their faces to the light. They might have been a tribe of ancient people, falling to the ground at the mention of their gods—or were they large children, gathered around a virtual rocking chair for story time?

David Ferriero grinned over their heads from the sidelines. A fresh crowd for the old library, new, alive, and up-to-date, playing with new media. *That's* the future of this library.

11.
WHAT'S WORTH SAVING?

"Just by the grace of God, really, did this collection survive."

_____

Who Do You Love?

When Toni Morrison's home in Grand View-on-Hudson, New York, burned down in 1993, a breathless *New York Times* article barely mentioned her adult son, who was there when a flying ember burst into flames and who tried in vain to extinguish it. The headline did not read TONI MORRISON'S SON SPARED IN CHRISTMAS FIRE. It read TONI MORRISON'S MANUSCRIPTS SPARED IN CHRISTMAS FIRE.

The fire was both alarming and ironic, the *Times* declared. Two weeks after she collected the Nobel Prize, "a writer's greatest honor, Ms. Morrison was subjected to what might have been a writer's greatest nightmare: the possible destruction of a large portion of her irreplaceable original manuscripts."

That's literary license, I assume; surely a worse nightmare would be the death by fire of her only child. But in diminishing the human in this story, the newspaper kept a tight focus on the manuscripts, only a few of which were in the house. You could boil this story down to a line: a little bit of water damage from fire hoses was sustained by a small number of manuscripts stored in a Nobel Prize winner's second home, which, by the way, was gutted. The whole piece was an excuse to read about Toni Morrison's papers, one of the great archival prizes still floating around out there. Never mind the son, the old house, even the fire. The real story was: Where will Toni send her papers? Where will Toni send her papers? Toni! Her papers! *Where will she send them?!*

Howard Dodson, chief of the New York Public Library's Schomburg Center for Research in Black Culture and a friend of Morrison's, admitted to the *Times* that he and the author had had informal talks about her donating some of those precious manuscripts of *Beloved* and *Song of Solomon* and *The Bluest Eye* to the Schomburg, but she hadn't committed. Not yet, maybe not ever. "The whole world wants her papers," Dodson acknowledged.

She has been judged in the company of Hemingway, Steinbeck, Saul Bellow, and Sinclair Lewis.

She won the prize that went to Beckett, Shaw, Sartre, Camus, Solzhenitsyn.

She's on the same immortal international list as Gabriel García Márquez, Thomas Mann, Isaac Bashevis Singer, Wole

Soyinka, Seamus Heaney, Günter Grass, Czesław Miłosz, and so on, and so on . . . you get the idea.

Her archives are gold. Her grocery list is gold. Some cheesy detective novel (she reads such novels for relaxation while she's writing her own books), complete with her thumbprints and dog-ears, is hot property. The sentence she was composing long ago when her son, then a toddler, threw up on the paper and she scrawled right through his vomit—well, maybe you'd toss it out with the coffee grounds and junk mail, but I promise you, that nasty scrap is worth a mint, and every archivist knows it.

The whole world wanted Norman Mailer's papers, too, but they went to the Harry Ransom Humanities Research Center at the University of Texas at Austin, all twenty thousand pounds of them, from the forty thousand letters to every version of each of his books, with one little exception (a draft of his first book, *The Naked and the Dead*). Mailer wrote more than forty books, many of them critically acclaimed best-sellers, in multiple genres over more than six decades, won everything but the Nobel Prize, and considered himself the peer of Tolstoy and Dostoyevsky. Maybe he wasn't as big as Tolstoy, but he was big.

The thing about archives is they need to go somewhere where they'll be preserved and remain accessible to scholars; and they really ought to end up somewhere that makes sense geographically. You don't expect the papers of the Harlem Renaissance to go to Indiana. The only connection to Texas that Mailer seemed to have, though, according to his *New York Times* obituary, was that during his stoned and drunken years in the fifties, he used to affect a variety of accents: British, Irish, gangster, and, yes, Texan.

Mailer had a long-winded answer for why he disappointed the libraries of Harvard, where he went to school; Brooklyn, where he grew up and lived for most of his eighty-four years; and New York City, a place where he'd left his mark not only culturally but politically as well, when he ran for mayor on a platform promising to declare it the fifty-first state. "In 1944, I came out of Fort Bragg an artillery replacement and was sent to the 112th Regimental Combat Team, originally from San Antonio but now in the Philippines," he wrote. "There I was converted into an infantry rifleman. So I got to know a fair amount about Texas over the next year. And Texans. Most of them were dirt-poor and damn tough. (For years afterward in New York, when trouble was brewing on the street, I would do my best to talk in a Texas accent.)

"To this, I can add a splendid few days I spent in Austin as a lecturer back in the very early '60s, and I do remember the university as one of the most exciting and open campuses I ever visited."

So faking a Texas accent really *was* part of it. His excuse was a stretch—or should we call this *rationalizing on a preposterous scale*? Not that there was anything wrong with the Harry Ransom Humanities Research Center at the University of Texas. On the contrary, it is a golden mountain, with a collection built ambitiously by Harry Huntt Ransom, and ambitiously supplemented by archivist Tom Staley, a man who rustles up sponsors when he finds a worthy prize, and delivers, time and again. So far, the Center holds papers by Jorge Luis Borges (a great writer *and* a great librarian), James Joyce, Isaac Bashevis Singer, Graham Greene, and Woodward and Bernstein, to mention a few. So many British authors were selling their papers to the Ransom Center that the archivists of Britain and Ireland organized the Group for Literary Archives and Manuscripts (GLAM) to counter the "wealthy overseas institutions with their hunger for archives and manuscripts of literatures other than their own, above all in English." They meant Texas, mainly. As an anonymous British archivist muttered in the *Guardian*: "Two things are inevitable, death and Texas."

Norman Mailer's papers went to the Ransom Center because the Texans offered him $2.5 million for his stash.

So what? They were his to give or sell. But this might explain why everyone got so excited about the fire licking at Toni Morrison's scraps.

The differences between the kings and the beggars in the writing world are vast: Toni Morrison's and Norman Mailer's letters are worth something and, published or not, donated or sold for vast sums, will be collected and treasured by highly trained archivists, cataloged, kept in climate-controlled rooms in expensive, acid-free boxes, scrutinized by scholars who will in turn be scrutinized by archivists watching them with squinty, suspicious eyes to make sure they don't deface, alter, or steal these precious written remnants of literary originality.

As a young editor, I used to comb *Esquire* magazine's slush pile for publishable stories by the unknown, or relatively unknown—or at any rate, unpursued—writers. Once I opened one that had a cigarette taped to it. "Have a smoke on me," the letter said, in a lunatic scrawl. My desperate, rejected correspondent had his letter, tobacco drifting from its taped cigarette, tossed in the trash.

There was another brown manila envelope that clawed its way out of the *Esquire* mailbag: my name and address were written in dark marker, and plastered across the top, the sides, and the back, were multiple bold notices, all proclaiming *FRIEND OF BILL SCHULZ!!!!* in scary handwriting. Schulz, a poet I'd known in graduate school, had alerted me to a writer living in his town's dump who seemed to have real talent. He told her I was expecting her manuscripts, but that's how impenetrable the glossy magazine must have seemed to her. The envelope and the letter inside were as disturbed and disturbing as those from Have a Smoke on Me. Her stories, however, were terrific, though not, perhaps, for a men's magazine like *Esquire*. I sent her on to a literary magazine, which published her, and they sent her on to a book editor, and who knows how many more people passed her along, but soon enough, four of her novels, most famously, *The Beans of Egypt, Maine*, were ushered into print. I wish I hadn't thrown away Carolyn Chute's letter (like the

envelope, emblazoned *FRIEND OF BILL SCHULZ!!!!*)—
not because of its financial worth, which in spite of her success, might not amount to much, though who knows?—but
because she is a singular and eloquent voice in our culture,
a woman who does indeed live in a garbage dump with her
husband, fires AK-47 rifles, and organizes protests for the
disaffected poor. The letter was a piece of evidence from her
extraordinary life. Someone could study it, use it to trace
her path out of obscurity or shed light on her body of work.
It could illuminate rural poverty in the late twentieth century. At the least, it would be another glimpse behind the
library shelf of the effort and serendipity and wild stories
involved in the process of amplifying the literary voice.

I came across the science-fiction writer Joseph V. Hamburger's
papers in a one-day workshop for archivists in "Managing Literary Manuscripts." The archivists in attendance worked in
the collections of research and university libraries, or for cor-
porations; one worked for a prominent architect, processing
his papers as he generated them. Another offered this tongue-
in-cheek job description: "I read other people's mail."

Near the end of the workshop, the two instructors divided
the class into teams and distributed files of raw literary material for us to identify, arrange, and describe. I was with the
team that got some letters and draft manuscripts of the work
of Tennessee Williams. This was exciting, even though we
were working with color facsimiles and even though our job
didn't involve reading what was actually written on these pages

(if you were doing archival work, you were supposed to skim them just enough to be able to write the finding aids, the breadcrumbs that could lead someone to it). I was impressed by how challenging it was to lay a path to an item for others to follow, to try to anticipate the researchers' questions. The difficulties were structural—how were these letters to be organized in the context of the collection? Where should it fit so the most people could find it? Where did it intellectually and organically make sense? These letters had been stuck between the pages of a draft of *The Night of the Iguana*, so maybe it made sense to group them with the manuscript, instead of in a file with Williams's miscellaneous correspondence.

There were three letters, from three dates early in 1961. Here's how the University of Delaware's Special Collections described them: "Three TLSs [typed letters, signed] from Tennessee Williams to the actress Katharine Hepburn in which he attempts to persuade her to play the role of Hannah Jelkes. The three letters are similar in content, and it appears Williams never sent the first two letters but only the final one for which he retained the photocopy which is present here."

There was a feeling in our group that we were getting privileged glimpses into a famous writer's backstage life, as evidenced by typos, coffee stains, and gossip. Of course these letters were worth saving. Tennessee Williams had been a searing writer who had animated generations of actors with words that grabbed his audience by the throat. He had imagined Katharine Hepburn as the prim, unmarried, impoverished Jelkes. Instead, Margaret Leighton got the role and won a Tony for it. A bit of theatrical history turned on these documents.

Other teams in the workshop got a folder of Gregory Corso's letters and poems, and a stack of Ishmael Reed's papers to process. The last team got a file (a song, a short story, a news clipping of a letter to the editor, and several poems, including one scrawled on a manila folder) from the writer Joseph V. Hamburger. The Williams, Corso, and Reed papers had come from the holdings of the University of Delaware, where L. Rebecca Johnson Melvin, one of our instructors, worked as an archivist. Her copresenter came from Penn State, but the Joseph V. Hamburger papers weren't from those archives, which boast early papers of Ernest Hemingway's, a play of John Updike's, and the John O'Hara collection. Susan Hamburger brought Joseph V. Hamburger's papers from her and Joe's house.

Not many people have heard of Joe Hamburger, even science-fiction fans. That's because Hamburger never actually published any of his sci-fi stories. He wasn't unpublished as a writer—articles, essays, poems, even a couple of encyclopedia entries found their way into print—but like most of us who call ourselves writers, he mainly collected rejection slips. Or, rather, he moved on to the next idea, the next piece, the next file, and his wife collected the rejection slips (and everything else besides).

I thought it was intriguing of Sue Hamburger to use a regular writer to demonstrate archival practices, but I was just as happy to be working on one of the celebrities' papers. Somewhere along the line, though, in our subsequent correspondence, I came to value her approach. I realized that it wasn't just convenience or pride on her part to bring along the literary archives of her husband, obscure as he might have been. It had been a deliberate strategy to show us that the tools of archiving were not only for Nobel and Pulitzer winners and MacArthur fellows. They were for anybody any of us thought worth saving.

And who is worth saving? Ah, that's the question. Certainly we are worth saving ourselves, whoever we are, if only for our family's sake. If we are helping build or create something, save a town landmark, fight for freedom, launch a field of study; if we survive a disaster or witness a miracle—if we do anything with our life besides watch television—we might want to document it somehow and save the evidence. Then again, forget that qualifier; someone who did nothing but watch TV might be able to tell us a great deal about the history of television in the twenty-first century. We are all living history, and it's hard to say now what will be important in the future. One thing's certain, though: if we throw it away, it's gone.

Sue Hamburger gave me good advice when I wrote to her about saving my work and my friends'. We should use open-source software anytime we have a choice. She warned us against saving text files in Word, for instance, and urged us to use instead the generic (and free) rich text format (rtf). Proprietary programs like Word go out of date quickly, she pointed out, and there's no guarantee a company will stay in business or feel an obligation to keep information readable into the future. However we organized our files, we should keep notes about the reasons behind our decisions. Oh—and if we were to be signing any books, we shouldn't use gel pens; their ink deteriorates. We should invest in a good archival-quality pen.

My e-mails were short and fractured, Sue Hamburger's long, carefully composed, and jammed with news of her activities. She had a high-maintenance home: five cats, gardens, a pool. She was working on a book about literary archiving with her copresenter Melvin. She read voraciously, and after reading my book about obituaries, lamented that she didn't have time to keep up with obits around the world. She might have tried, too, except her husband, the writer, was in a hospital in Hershey, Pennsylvania, two hours from home, recovering from multiple surgeries related to bladder cancer. "The poor guy is like an old car—fix one thing and something else goes wrong." Twice a week, she left her job at the Penn State University Libraries and took a two-hour bus ride from State College to sit by his hospital bed. On weekends, she drove there, and on the way back, swung by the Salvation Army in Camp Hill to buy used clothing that she then sold to vintage stores, a little business she and Joe ran on the side. They had another business, as well—had she mentioned this?—as spies for a music licensing company, visiting restaurants, dance clubs, stadiums, and other public places to document the music that was broadcast, the first step in policing music copyrights. I pictured her, energetically gathering the world's loose ends, old clothes, old papers, dispersed music, and putting them in their rightful place. Salvaging.

I also pictured her trapped on a bus, her honey-colored hair so long she could sit on it, shirt neatly tucked into her jeans, being driven hours down a winter highway, to sit vigil next to her precious husband, the writer.

I went away for Christmas, and by the time we caught up, there was an obituary in my in-box for Joseph Victor "Jersey Joe" Hamburger.

The Hamburgers' house was on an acre at the corner of two roads in farm country, a raised brick ranch with white pillars in front. The side yard held the two organic garden plots. In the back was the hot tub and the aboveground pool, fenced behind the chain links of a former dog run. A development of mansions was rising up across the road, but otherwise the country felt unspoiled. The university was ten minutes away, past bucolic scenes—long stretches of undulating land, a pond surrounded by native grasses, the vista of Mount Nitanny.

The cat boxes sat right inside the front door, accommodating five cats, mostly variations on Siamese. The air was humid with cats. There were cat signs on the coat closet (*No outfit is complete without cat hair!*), by the front door (*Don't let the cat out no matter what it tells you!*), and in the kitchen (*Spoiled rotten cats live here*). The interior was a kaleidoscope of cats, cats rendered in oil, ceramic, iron, wood, real cats prowling the acid-green carpet of the living room, fake cats on the walls and bookshelves and tables and piano.

Back in Hamburger's bedroom, the mattress rested on the floor, in readiness for new bedroom furniture and a new paint job. There were bags of stuffed animals to give away, along with several old chests of drawers, smeared with putty where Joe had begun to fix the gouges and scratches. "You wouldn't believe what I've already taken out of this house," Sue said. Joe was a compulsive shopper who haunted the thrift stores, originally to supplement his cool musician wardrobe with leather coats and funky shirts. He'd bring back clothes and other things, too, space toys and model cars, cat tchotchkes, books, and furniture. At some point his therapist suggested he start reselling the vintage clothes. The basement is stuffed with the remnants of that business, which Sue had stepped in and organized. "Joe wasn't practical. He couldn't find things, had no idea whether he was making any money, so I designed a tag that went on each garment as it came in, coded for what type of garment it was, like jacket or pants, and how much it cost, and sorted them into bins."

On this chilly March day, three months after his death, Susan Hamburger was surrounded by stacks of her husband's work. She was going to use her professional skills to decide what to preserve among the scrawled paper place mats, the copied flyers, the stories and poems and lyrics and letters and self-help articles that Joe wrote and she rescued. Her plan was to organize all of it, sort it into acid-free archival files and boxes, write catalog descriptions and develop finding aids, then donate the processed archives to his alma mater, Rutgers University. Sue had called a colleague there and told him of her intentions. His response? "Dead air on the line." No matter. If Rutgers didn't want it, she'd find someplace that would.

Sue and Joe had met when they were students at Monmouth College (now Monmouth University) in New Jersey when he tried to pick her up at the music store where she'd gone to buy a left-handed twelve-string guitar. "He was so smart. He knew so many things." Within weeks they were living together; they married on Valentine's Day 1968. Music was a bond, as was a shared resentment over their parents' failures: Sue's father had died when she was sixteen, leaving the family impoverished, and her mother drank, and Joe had been brought up by Communists, so preoccupied with politics and other people's rights he felt abandoned. Joe and Sue agreed never to have children themselves. They got through school (Joe with a bachelor's in psychology, and Sue with two master's degrees, including a master's in library science, and a doctorate in American history), and began moving around the country, following Sue's employment. They almost divorced while living in Connecticut, where Joe couldn't find work and began drinking. Instead, he sobered up, went into treatment, and earned a master's in rehabilitation counseling, which he was able to practice off and on for years. Mainly, though, and especially after his health began to decline, he wrote and he played music.

Sue separated piles of his poetry from his music. "I can identify the poetry, and I know the songs: the poetry never rhymes and the songs always do. If I turn this collection over to somebody else, they wouldn't know the difference, necessarily.

"He couldn't handle the practical aspects of writing. Joe took rejection personally. He would find a science-fiction editor who encouraged him, then the publication would collapse or the editor would leave.

"In his lifetime, I was proofreading everything he did and, initially, with the poetry and the short stories, I paid a typist to make a clean copy. I had a folder of the master, then made copies to send out. I put them in the top of my closet so everything was organized—and then he got to them. And one time he decided he was going to revise the stories. . . . Trying to find the original copy, the master, is going to be fun. Normally with a literary person, they'll have different drafts, an original, then they'll edit that, retype or rewrite, or cut and paste—it's a messy, messy process. The creative person isn't thinking of organization."

Sue kept the flyers and local newspaper announcements of appearances by "Jersey Joe," which is what Joe called himself when he strapped on his guitar and covered Bruce Springsteen, or played original songs like "eBay Blues (Selling Memories)," and she also kept a handwritten list of performances they did together dating back to 1967. She showed me one of Joe's claims to fame: the album cover of Dylan's *Bringing It All Back Home*, which had a photograph on the back prominently featuring Joe's handsome face in a crowd around the singer, and the academic paper he wrote about Springsteen, who had gone to the same high school he had and been bullied by the same crowd. Joe speculated about the psychology that drove him to embrace in his lyrics the greasers who used to torment him.

Sue tossed out the ephemera, the buttons and magazine clippings of bands Joe liked; she made copies of the essays he had published in newspapers, then threw out the originals. "Newspaper yellows and disintegrates, and what we care about with this collection is the content." She pulled letters out of envelopes and, if the letters were dated and had a return address, she tossed the envelopes. She had already written a biographical note for the collection that included when and where Joe had lived; that would be useful for dating items with a return address. She ditched the rusty paper clips and pried out staples. She separated versions of manuscripts with legal-sized pieces of acid-free paper, so they could also function as bookmarks. "You leave one side open in the file, unless the paper has been de-acidified. Paper still breathes. We used to encase the documents in Mylar, but that cooked them. Only use Mylar, now known as Melinex; other plastic, if you can smell it, it's not good."

The sorting seemed simple, until you actually started doing it. "Here are two different versions of the same story, one with a little intro that isn't on the other copy. What the archivist has to do is figure out which came first. In some cases you might not know. Draft A, draft B, both undated. You leave that to the scholar studying the writer to figure out.

"You have to make a decision when you're processing, How much effort do you go through to organize the collection item by item? How important is the person? Since it's my husband, and it's before I'm giving it to an archive, and I have plenty of time to deal with it, I'll go through and reorganize these pages."

There were only two rooms in Sue's house off limits to the cats, and one was the office. Sue shooed them away, but when we squeezed through the door, a cat managed to streak past our legs and burrow among the wires behind one of the desks. Sue got on her hands and knees to drag the cat out while I looked around. We were standing in a museum of technology. "I have every computer I ever owned. Some work with the scanner and the camera, some don't." She had connectivity as ancient as some of the machines, a dial-up connection through the university.

"Joe took to the computer like a duck to water. It was so exciting, to write all this stuff and go back to make changes. That's a difficult thing for an archivist, authors who don't have multiple drafts to see. Of course with the computer, open a new file and you change the date; you don't know when something was written, and so many of his files weren't named. He'd hit 'save,' and the file name would be our address.

"I'll go through these things and print out what I can find. That's the best way to save them." The floppies and CDs were time bombs, unreadable without computer forensics, except in a room like this, where you could insert them in the computer that created them.

We moved back to the open kitchen to sit at the round kitchen table, stacked with books and periodicals and the box containing Joe's ashes. Sue made us herbal tea—no alcohol in this house. She fussed with the sound system in the living room, and put on Joe's songs, and his rich baritone filled the room with a love song for Susie: deft folk guitar moves, nimble lyrics, and a warm, slightly slurry voice.

"Joe came to all the archival conferences with me. He joined one of the archival groups and got interested in oral histories.

He was going to write about growing up as a 'red-diaper baby,' the child of Communists," Sue said. "Gertrude Dubrovsky grew up in the same Jewish community he grew up in, and wrote a book and made a film about it: *The Land Was Theirs: Jewish Farmers in the Garden State*. She interviewed his parents, and us, too. Her research and notes are in the Farmingdale Collection at Rutgers."

So Joe is already there in the Rutgers archives, and of all the stories he had to tell, maybe being the son of Jewish Communists raising chickens in New Jersey is the most compelling, and his papers belong with the papers of others who documented this subculture. But just in case his literary work or his rock-and-roll legacy is deemed of interest, Sue will be ready. She thought his work was worth saving, so it was saved. That's the story of all archives. "I'll say to Rutgers, 'Here is an alum who has been published, he has interesting writings, he's connected to their other holdings. Someone can get something out of this. Want it?'"

He spent his adult life looking for a home for his writing. Why would that stop just because he's gone?

The Great Boxing Archive

Librarian David Smith put in an appearance at the ALA's 2008 midwinter conference, but he left the meetings, panels, speeches, get-togethers, and exhibits to his wife. He hung out where the husbands of librarians hang: in a sports bar a block from the conference center, where most of the televisions in a bank behind the bar were tuned to a Colts–Chargers playoff game (though one featured guys playing pool). It was three in the afternoon. Smith had cornered a table, a prime viewing spot, covered with newspapers, anchored by a bottle of beer.

"Did anybody recognize you?" I asked. A few weeks earlier, not long after his holiday party for writers at the New York Public Library, the *New York Times* article about him had appeared. Sam Roberts' piece, which described him as "the Virgil of the stacks," and "librarian to the stars," had lit up the library blogs.

Smith grinned. "Yeah, a few. One guy said, 'Go, reference!'"

Debbi Smith was chairing a committee meeting that afternoon—she is a force in collection development for academic libraries—and then she was dragging David to dinner with a database vendor. Smith got gloomy just thinking about it. "All these people talk about is libraries," he said. Not books; that would have been fine; just libraries. Then he came to life, remembering something he'd wanted to share. "Hey, did you see Hank Kaplan's obituary? The guy with the incredible boxing archives? I couldn't tell you the story before, but now I can."

Sometime in the mid-eighties, Smith started dreaming about a place where he could go to see the classic fights, read about the great boxers, hang out and talk about them. A cable channel devoted to classic fights soon debuted, and his dream lost its urgency. But Smith still nurtured the idea of a library, a club, a space devoted to boxing. Scholars of boxing were not being served. True fight fans, a shrinking but dedicated constituency, deserved more.

Meanwhile, in the course of his reference work, Smith got to know the authors of several boxing books, David Margolick, Ron Fried, Jeremy Schaap. One night, Margolick told him about these incredible archives. Hank Kaplan was a boxing fan whose suburban Miami house was stuffed with clippings, posters, and books about boxing. Half a million photographs. The history of the best fighters, but also the history of the others, including the worst fighter in the world, a guy aptly named Joe Grim who lost ninety-one fights and won only six. The story of women in boxing, bareknuckle fighting, animals in the ring. *Sports Illustrated*, ESPN, HBO, Showtime, all of them used Hank Kaplan's phenomenal memory and his archives. Kaplan told a reporter in the nineties: "Even when I was 16 or 17, I said there's got to be some way to remember them. If someone were to ask me why I keep the archives, I guess that's what I'd say: Someone has to be charged with remembering them."

In his eighties, Kaplan began thinking about selling his collection of *fistic arcana*. He put a price tag of $300,000 on it, "which was *very* reasonable," Smith said. "We're talking huge, irreplaceable." (Smith had never actually seen the archives, but he was a librarian; he knew.) Smith floated the idea of buying it to someone in archives acquisitions at the New York Public Library, but the collection was too big, too specialized.

So when Smith read a newspaper article about Alan Dershowitz donating his papers to the Brooklyn College Library, and saw, buried deep in the piece, the detail that the archivist receiving those papers liked to box, he was dumbstruck. What do you know—a boxing archivist. Smith immediately shot an e-mail to the guy, Anthony Cucchiara, and began inviting him to readings by the boxing writers.

That's what the boxing archives needed: a boxing archivist. That's how the Kaplan archives would come to New York.

"How can you tell the archivists from the librarians?" a young librarian in Brooklyn was asked. "Different gang colors," she joked. You can offend either profession by confusing or con-flating them, but I couldn't pick the archivist out of a police lineup of librarians. Except for the tattooed ones, all of them looked like people I'd known at Oberlin.

I might not be able to distinguish them, but I knew the difference. In spite of Smith's efforts to save these archives, he was, like most librarians, a finder. Librarians were find-ers. Archivists were keepers. Smith could find anything. Tony Cucchiara would keep anything.

Cucchiara found his calling as a student intern in the ar-chives of St. Francis College, a small men's school in Brooklyn Heights. "The original town records of Brooklyn were being thrown out by the county clerk's office back in the sixties. I would go with the archivists and Dumpster-dive to retrieve these things—that's how I got into it. It's almost like a fever."

Not long after Cucchiara came to work at Brooklyn Col-lege, an English professor called his desk. Someone on her street had thrown out a steam trunk, "filled to the brim with the diaries, letters, mountain-climbing journals, and the photographs of Annie Peck, one of the first woman mountain climbers in 1905 and 1910." Originally, it seemed, Peck had sent the trunk from her home in Rhode Island to a Brooklyn writer who planned to write her biography. He died before he got around to it. The people cleaning his house figured the papers for junk and left them on the curb . . . and now the Annie Peck papers live in the Brooklyn College archives.

Tony Cucchiara is in his late fifties, and fit, somewhere between a lightweight and a welterweight. The only clue to his age are the carved parentheses around his mouth. He spars three times a week at Gleason's Gym. He has been the archivist at Brooklyn College for over twenty years, and only once did he pay for a collection, when he bought the papers of William Alfred, a playwright and alumnus who corresponded with a host of literary and stage figures, from Robert Lowell to Faye Dunaway. At a time when significant archives command big money, Cucchiara simply asked Alan Dershowitz to donate his papers. If not for Brooklyn College, Dershowitz felt, he would have been a dry cleaner like his father instead of a lawyer; donating his papers was a great way to say thanks. The *Times* picked up the story; David Smith clipped it; and soon Cucchiara was sitting in Jimmy's Corner, a Times Square bar run by Jimmy Glenn, a former boxer and cutman, conspiring with Smith's gang to bring the Hank Kaplan archives to New York.

The Boxing Hall of Fame is in upstate New York, four and a

half hours from the city, and most of the fights these days take place in Las Vegas. But for this group of boxing fans, the history of boxing and its multiethnic boxers was centered in New York City, and Kaplan himself started out in Brooklyn—they had lots of reasons his papers should end up there. And here they were—boxing writers, a librarian, and an archivist—all willing to raise hundreds of thousands of dollars and swear eternal guardianship of the collection. Its size would tax the space and labor resources of most archives, but Cucchiara's library had recently been renovated, and he directed a program that trained students across the disciplines in archival studies. He had room to hold all those papers and interns to help process them.

This was the plan: sportswriter Jeremy Schaap would be flying down to Florida for the Super Bowl and would swing by Kaplan's home in suburban Miami and shoot some footage. Then the group would have Kaplan's voice and presence and shots of some of his treasures—not to mention pictures of this house and garage stuffed to the rafters—to show potential investors. They particularly wanted to approach Robert De Niro, who won an Academy Award playing the boxer Jake LaMotta. When Schaap had to back out of the trip, Cucchiara stepped in. He flew to Miami in the spring of 2007, on his own dime, and shot three hours of footage for a short documentary on Hank Kaplan, *The Lord of the Ring*.

But before he and the others could approach De Niro or anyone else, Kaplan's health began to fail. Early in December, Cucchiara got a call from Kaplan's daughter. The eighty-eight-year-old boxing historian was dying, but he wanted

Cucchiara to know that the collection would be his. The public announcement appeared at the end of the appreciative and moving obituary of Kaplan that appeared in the *Washington Post*: the archives' next home would be Brooklyn College.

Forget the $300,000. All Cucchiara had to do was raise $10,000 to have an archival mover transfer the precious papers and photographs from Miami to Brooklyn.

It was probably just as well the group didn't get around to asking for De Niro's help. Kaplan had been a boxing writer as well as a collector, and he had blasted *Raging Bull* when it came out. "A lingering question as I exited the theater was why Robert De Niro, a great actor, to be sure, studied for so long the boxing style and technique of Jake LaMotta, only to depict a boxer so unlike the Bronx Bull that to identify him would be impossible"—after which Kaplan had given a short and authoritative lesson in why LaMotta had been so great and why we should care that someone got it wrong.

Kaplan had not been trained formally in the archival arts, though he had taught himself some skills, but he had been a biologist before he retired; he knew how to structure things. Still, the collection he assembled had been kept for decades in a frame house and garage in the hurricane belt, and Hurricane Andrew had torn the roof off in the early nineties. The house was unguarded for two months after Kaplan died, and his obituaries referred to his collection as "priceless." In fact, it was worth far more than the original asking price; it was appraised for $2.94 million. That thieves didn't get there before the moving van was another miracle. "Just by the grace of God, really, did this collection survive," Cucchiara marveled.

Certainly serendipity and luck were at play in this story. What if a hurricane had torn off not just the roof but the rest of the building, too? What if the librarian reading the newspaper hadn't turned the page? What if Cucchiara had not gone to Miami himself to meet Kaplan? What if a sports memorabilia seller had swooped in, bought the lot, and held an auction? What if the moving van had crashed? But you could make yourself crazy thinking like that. What if Hank Kaplan had suffered brain damage in his single pro fight, and reading made him dizzy, and he had never collected a scrap?

What endures, if luck endured with it, was something real and true, a history of a primal sport across time and cultures, vivid with stories. And the key element, the most important by far, was the last *what if*: What if one person hadn't bothered to keep all this in the first place? Because without that keeper, the rest hardly mattered.

Digital Scraps

Hank Kaplan lived in a simpler world, archivally speaking. Every night, he sat down and cut up the newspapers and filed photographs and wrote ten or twelve letters to correspondents around the world, exchanging boxing news and trading artifacts. He received so many letters, that he began throwing them away, unless they came from Muhammad Ali or Angelo Dundee, the legendary cornerman. He still managed to collect a massive amount of paper, but he never got into computers; he didn't have shirt boxes full of floppy discs.

What about the Hank Kaplans of today?

What if I had something I wanted to capture from the Web—a snapshot of every headline that ran the day a baby was born; or a file of every photo of Salma Hayek, to see how often she smiled. Or maybe I wanted to collect stories about viruses that spread like viruses. How would I collect them all? What if I wanted to be like Hank Kaplan and document, say, the winners and the losers of *American Idol*, instead of boxing matches? Or, more likely, what if I wanted to save the spontaneous outpourings and arias of grief posted in the wake of a tragic event—the Virginia Tech massacre, or the sudden death of an admired writer. How could I save such stories for myself and others? How could I save them, and organize them, so they were useful into the future?

I had learned the hard way that saving links wasn't good enough; they led to "Page Error" as often as not, to places where places on the Web used to be. The librarian who had first shown me how to make screenshots had opened up a world for me, but before long, I had a desktop cluttered with screenshots. I didn't know how to arrange them—by date? subject? author? Should I keep the blog posts separate from the work in quality publications like *Newsweek*? Then where would I put *Newsweek*'s blogs? When I tried to share the screenshots via e-mail, other people couldn't open them unless they were using the same browser I did. I was making a noble effort, but it was mostly useless. That wasn't the idea.

I studied books about digital archives. It was hard to con-
centrate on them, so I started reading them on the treadmill.
This had the advantage of preventing me from making a lot of
notes and clutter, while keeping oxygen flowing to my brain.
The books were as weighty as manuals, and, like websites that
lead only to more websites, free of simple, readable content;
their pages were all about principles of organization, arranged
in bullet style, like PowerPoint presentations, only longer. But
I could never find anything that told me what I personally
could do about the looming nightmare of lost digital data,
besides make a lot of copies in a lot of different formats. I
couldn't find a Dummies book for amateur digital archivists.

I tacked questions at the back of every interview—how
could I personally create a digital archive? The librarians and
archivists I consulted were all terribly concerned about the
burgeoning Web, pages disappearing from sites shutting down,
the threat of data corruption, and censorship. Everyone knew
stories of old blogs or photograph collections disappearing—
everybody heard a whoosh in the air. "We're talking about
terabytes, terabytes of data, of hundreds of thousands of man-
hours of work, crafted by people, an anthropological bonanza
and a critical part of online history, wiped out because someone
had to show that they were cutting costs," one blogger wrote
after the disappearance of another clutch of social-networking
sites. How could I capture even a few specks of this data? I
wanted to reach my hand into the speeding, spinning ether of
the Internet and pluck out pages, and save them in an elegant
format that would be useful in time.

The digital librarian Brewster Kahle had looked at the Internet in 1994 and thought, Somebody ought to save this stuff. Kahle put up his own money and formed the Internet Archive, and he has been crawling the Web ever since with his team of archivists, taking snapshots as fast as the technology permits. (If someone objects on copyright grounds, the Internet Archive simply removes the page.) Now anyone can go to archive.org, and find billions of old webpages on its "Wayback Machine"— not everything, not by a long shot, but such a tremendous file, it can be searched only by Web address. You can't type in *living Mouseketeers* and see that slice of history. You can, however, type in *amazon.com* and see snapshots of a page from 1998, evidence of how very long ago 1998 was ($100 rebate for buying a magenta-pink RAZR phone). "Internet libraries can change the content of the Internet from ephemera to enduring artifacts of our political and cultural lives," the archive declares.

It is a fantastic resource, and Kahle had stepped in while libraries and museums dawdled. But you couldn't (yet) use it to build a digital archive of bloodied-up boxers or young writers' tributes to John Updike. And what will the future be missing if the present doesn't have a Hank Kaplan here and there, squirreling away the scraps of his or her particular obsession?

As it happened, I had a source who had helped develop a prototype for a free, do-it-yourself, Web archiving tool. "How do you collect stuff on the Web so that it's useful down the road?" Josh Greenberg of the New York Public Library did not have to puzzle this out for a second. Before this job, Greenberg had been working at the Center for History and New Media at George Mason University, where he helped develop a prototype of the free Firefox extension Zotero. It would save a snapshot of any webpage I wanted, and all sorts of other information, as well. "Say you're on Amazon looking for a book," Greenberg explained. "One way of remembering that book would be, jot down the title. Another way would be, type all the information about it—the title, author, publisher, and so on—into a bibliographic program. But it turns out, we can grab that data automatically if we are crafty about how we get it. In Zotero, you go to an Amazon page and a little icon pops up in the menu bar that looks like a book. You click it and it pulls in all the information about that book that Amazon has. It's spectacular." Bingo—Archives for Dummies!

Amateurs and enthusiasts like me have a lot to contribute, Greenberg added; we're witnessing and sometimes even shaping history. In fact, if Greenberg ever gets a chance to catch his breath, he's going to write a book about the rise of amateurs and enthusiasts who end up contributing their expertise and more to our culture.

"It needs to be as easy to set up an online archive as it is to set up a blog," he said, and suddenly, all over town, bells tolled and horns honked and even the pigeons sang. Such a simple, lucid summary of my search. Like the best librarians and archivists, Greenberg had shown me how to figure out what I wanted to do, then pointed me toward the answer. I wanted to *keep* something from the Web that I could *find* again later. I wanted to keep what I read there alive.

Josh Greenberg's work at George Mason had been part of an initiative funded by the Arthur P. Sloan Foundation called Exploring and Collecting History Online. "We were building websites to collect stories. The first major success was the project called the September 11th Digital Archive. Within weeks of 9/11, my colleague, Dan Cohen, set up a site that asked people for their stories or their photographs. People uploaded all sorts of stuff. One of my favorites was the chart of a guy's heart rate; he happened to be jogging across the Brooklyn Bridge and had his heart monitor on. You actually see these two spikes. It's an amazing visual artifact."

After the team gathered all these items, it donated the lot to the Library of Congress, where the staff has been working on digital archives since 1994. One of the library's digital conversion specialists, Liz Madden, wrote that they took on this project because it "provided a practical, real-world example of what digital donations might look like in the future." The staff figured out how to catalog it, and now the September 11th Digital Archive—snapshots of newspapers, emergency websites, personal letters and photos, and even the stress test, the stuff of our history, the first born-digital collection at the Library of Congress—lives on the Web.

The Library of Congress made another foray into digital history when it began an experiment with Flickr in 2008, posting a fraction of the million digitized photographs in its archives on that network and inviting the public to help identify the images. The Library of Congress/Flickr project was, from the beginning, a great success, attracting attention to the library's archives and leveraging the knowledge of the public in the freewheeling style of the Web; more than 3 million views were counted the first week alone. The tone on the library's blog was jubilant: "nothing short of astounding. You always hope for a positive reaction to something like this, but it has been utterly off the charts." Facts, memories, found photographers, long discussions about why hay bales are different shapes in different parts of the country, and a tremendous amount of goodwill have been generated by the project. One of the factors in its success, according to the library's final report, was due to the fact that "A venerable institution like the Library of Congress participating (and seemingly conversant) in a popular Web 2.0 space was unexpected and attracted attention."

The Library of Congress had taken some of its archives into the world, preserved them in new ways, and given them new life in the shared space of the commons. Immeasurable free publicity and free research help were the result. Not even one full-time worker had been budgeted and the cost of the library's Flickr Pro account was $24.95 a year. It was not much more than a Library 2.0 vision, pure and simple: Spread the gold, and trust the reader.

12.

THE BEST DAY

I was under the librarians' protection.
Civil servants and servants of civility, they had my back.

I approached the opening of the new Darien Library in Darien, Connecticut, not as an outsider who lived forty-five minutes away but as a welcome guest. Here was a public library that flung open its doors to people from beyond the town limits. A banner quote emblazoned its home page for a while—"I live in California, but I keep Darien Library's number in my phone for good answers to my questions." Imagine that!

It's true that without a Darien library card, I couldn't actually check out the laptops and GPS devices and Kindles available to local patrons. I couldn't take BlackBerry boot camp (what a shame). Nor could I read the *Wall Street Journal* online (database access is restricted by the providers)—though I could become a friend of their library for $300 and enjoy any and all of these privileges. Even as a mere piker and carpetbagger,

I was invited to register on their website and help myself to resources like podcast interviews with authors and staff-written reviews. And, most important, I was invited to consult their librarians. About anything! Their librarians would be happy to work for me. Any person in the universe can consult Darien's Ask a Librarian using the instant-messaging service, Meebo, on the library's website. It told you if the library was online, and warned you it might take a little while; but the weekend it opened, when the library was packed with hundreds of people, I tried this after I returned home and a librarian sent me the text of an article from the Darien paper in fifteen minutes. "*We're always thinking SERVICE,*" the website proclaimed. Reader, I was serviced.

This friendly embrace of anyone who walked through the door—or called, or used the instant-message service—was the mark of an evolved library. "The time soon will come when the idea of defining the clientele a library serves in very narrow, often geographically constrained terms will seem very quaint and old-fashioned," librarian Tom Peters wrote in a blog for the American Library Association. "Usage of information and information services has been going global since global information networks became widely used." His modest suggestion: "Perhaps a few forward-thinking library staffers, with the full support of their boards and their currently defined clientele, should openly declare that they serve the entire world, at least in theory." *At least in theory.* Is there any harm in that? In practice, we already see that all over the Web. And public libraries do, after all, hang signs that say "public."

The library blogs had been buzzing about Darien's opening for
months. The Darien site itself had a countdown clock keeping
track of the hours, minutes, even seconds till the new library
opened. Michael Stephens and others had been beating the
drum about the library's innovations and generosity in sharing
them. John Blyberg, assistant director for innovation and user
experience for the library, had been posting time-lapse videos
of the construction, bragging about the new surface-mounted
computer they were installing in the children's room that fit
into a tabletop and had a touch screen. He also unveiled on
the webpage a sweet, simple interface with their catalog, one
that allowed patrons to add their own tags to the catalog (*book
club possibility*, for instance, or *social studies extra credit*). The
next time the patrons used the catalog, they could log in, type
in *book club possibility*, and everything they marked with that
tag would pop up.

I'd caught the anticipation and wanted to be there for the
opening, but because of a glitch on their website, the old address floated on the bottom of the page with a MapQuest link
to the old library. Fortunately, I found the new site on Post
Road, a few blocks away, in time. I recognized the new building: red brick and glass, standing between life, in the form of
a greenhouse, on one side, and death, a veterans' cemetery, on
the other—rows of headstones standing guard from the Civil
War, the Spanish American War, and the World War, as the
headstones read, meaning the first.

Minutes before ten, according to the big clock on the tower

that rose in the middle of the building, a janitor swept the sidewalk under a blue ribbon stretched across the entrance. The 130 parking places in the back of the new library had been filled. Two policemen in knit caps and reflective gloves and vests stood by the entrance, prepared to direct the overflow. The place still had a raw construction feeling, with a pile of stones under tarp and visible edges on the squares of sod. Thirty degrees; the threat of snow was in the air this Saturday morning, January 10, 2009; nothing but bleak news from the front page to the weather forecast and the business news, especially in Darien, which *BusinessWeek* predicted would be the U.S. town hardest hit by the economic downturn.

And here were babies, children, teens, adults, seniors, some carrying stacks of books, crowded close and chattering and stamping their feet to keep warm in the plaza, though a few walked around to the front and, although the library hadn't yet officially opened, stepped inside to warm up (as it turned out, part of Darien Library's "extreme service" policy was letting people walk in anytime staff was on the premises, even when the staff was off-duty). "I was here with the senior men of Darien on Wednesday night," the man next to me confided. "There were thirty or forty of us who came to help dust and test the automatic checkout machines—and there were still carpenters working, and shrink wrap around all the furniture. It's really kind of miraculous."

Then the public-address system crackled to life, and we learned how the library was founded in 1894, moving from one rented space to another for more than fifty years before it

found a home on Leroy Avenue. There it had stayed for more
than fifty years, until now. New libraries don't just get built,
especially during a recession. Many people toiled to make it
happen, raising $24 million in the process. We cheered the
leader of the capital campaign, the environmental guru who
took a toxic-waste dump and turned it into an eco-friendly
building site, the state official who helped cut through red
tape, the architects of this quintessential New England space,
impressive yet modest—just right for the times.

It was a birthday party, it turned out. An elder of the town
who broke the ground for the new library, and almost single-
handedly (according to Darien Library's website) built the first
library, was celebrating his ninety-first birthday. That was the
entire reason, we learned, that the grand opening was scheduled for early January instead of, say, mid-June. So hundreds of
us shivered and sang "Happy Birthday" to Harold W. McGraw,
Jr., chairman emeritus of McGraw-Hill publishing, beaming in
his wheelchair. Once in a lifetime a community builds a library,
we were told. McGraw, though—he helped build two.

I was swept forward with the crush when the doors finally
opened. "I think those are the architects over there by the
door," a woman next to me said, excitement in her voice, and
when she finally reached them, she clasped the young men's
hands and exclaimed over the building's beauty. They seemed
almost embarrassed. "Go on in," they told her. "It's yours now."
In the vestibule, you could return books into a machine with
a conveyer belt that pitched down into the basement and was
visible through the glass: the inner workings of the library

revealed, a neat touch. There was a welcoming line of librarians, some of whom I recognized from the photos on the library's website (*Erica is starting Library School this fall! She's also a fig addict and notary. Pat is a dog lover and haunter of book shops everywhere. Ask her about the best in books on CD or Playaways*). I met Louise Berry, the visionary director, and the bloggers John Blyberg and Kate Sheehan, whom I'd been following from a distance.

I'd see the library in my own time that morning: the computer center in the basement, the teen room with kids drawing on the windows with markers, the art show, and the café. Upstairs, I'd see the self-checkout machines, the open, airy reading room, the sleek auditorium and screening room, the galleys overlooking the clean, spacious, orderly stacks. Information here doesn't seem to be exploding and out-of-control, but manageable and easy to find.

The librarians were friendly and helpful. *This is your place*, was the message. A child on his way to the treasure hunt in the children's room asked if he, too, could have one of those yellow hardhats the little people seem to be wearing and the librarian reached over and handed him one. "Help yourself!" And everywhere there were nooks and crannies, café tables to sit at or lounge chairs clustered by a window; a small meeting room under the eaves; chairs by the gas fireplace. Even in that crowd, it was possible to find a quiet spot to sit down.

I was overwhelmed by all this library business. I had been stuffing more and more information into my head, some of it digested, some not. The cataloging business, for instance—oh, the cataloging books that littered my house . . . ! That part of librarianship seemed so bloodless, but an awful lot of metaphoric blood was being shed. I just couldn't take it in. I regretted my human form briefly; it would be so much easier to drag and drop information into the brain as neatly as one dragged and dropped information on the computer. Perhaps I was suffering from a touch of *information sickness*? If I could weed out my thoughts . . .

There was one reliable cure I've found, a bit of the hair of the dog—the release in reading. Not a manual: something with a narrative. A chute built by a writer and waxed until the reader fell into it and skittered right to the end without stopping. The relief of being in someone else's hands. Yes, exactly: I needed to be under a spell.

I wandered across the austerely elegant stone floor down an aisle of newer books, and dropped onto a wood bench by a big window lit by winter light. I pulled the book closest to me off the shelf, *Wild Nights!* by Joyce Carol Oates, its subtitle a magnet for someone who loved old books: *Stories about the Last Days of Poe, Dickinson, Twain, James, and Hemingway.* And I fell down that chute, while the happy crowd buzzed just beyond the stacks. "EDickinsonRepliLuxe" is as strange a story as the strange writer tells. It's the future, perhaps the same future as in *Easy Travel to Other Planets.* A childless couple purchase an animatronic Emily Dickinson to live with them in their home. The creature spends most of her time hiding in her room, scribbling poems and reading, and slowly, steadily, the creepiness mounts, until the line between what we read and who we are blurs completely.

It didn't matter who I was, or what I did, or where I paid taxes, or how long I stayed. I'm sure it didn't matter if the book had RFID tags or a checkout card with a ladder of scrawled names, though tags were neat. I knew the librarians would help me figure out anything I needed to know later—This town is hurting economically, right? How many parking spaces in your lot? What do you call sign-making skills (wayfinding)? And which of your librarians likes figs?

I was under the librarians' protection. Civil servants and servants of civility, they had my back. They would be whatever they needed to be that day: information professionals, teachers, police, community organizers, computer technicians, historians, confidantes, clerks, social workers, storytellers, or, in this case, guardians of my peace.

They were the authors of this opportunity—diversion from the economy and distraction from snow, protectors of the bubble of concentration I'd found in the maddening world. And I knew they wouldn't disturb me until closing time.

Epilogue
Four Scenes
Washington, D.C.
June 2010

The librarian, not yet thirty years old, flashed her brilliant smile and shrugged. "Don't know yet," she said, shorthand for all that was on the table while New York's mayor and city council hammered out the budget that would affect the fate of the city's three library systems: New York, Brooklyn, and Queens. LIBRARIES "BIGGEST LOSER" IN CITY BUDGET, the headlines read, after the mayor proposed cutting city aid to libraries by 22 percent. The young librarian's employer, the Queens Public Library, had not waited to hear that perhaps two-thirds of this year's cuts would be restored by the council in negotiations. Instead, it had gone ahead and issued pink slips to 325 of its employees, and if it could eventually reinstate some of them, fine. The librarian had received notice that she would be laid off in ninety days, but it was still possible that the final budget would spare her job. She was spending the weekend in Washington, D.C., at the American Library Association's annual convention, in limbo, haunting the exhibits and meetings.

It would be one thing if the cuts were justified, but they had nothing to do with the needs of her patrons—demand for library services has skyrocketed during the recession—and nothing to do with the excellence of the library or her job performance. In fact, last year, *Library Journal* named the Queens Public Library system, with the largest circulation in the country, the best library in the United States. By all accounts, this young woman—conscientious, even inspired—was a great librarian, but three years did not give her enough seniority to protect her job. The librarian knew she was needed. Her teen room was packed. With colleagues across the city, she had organized an activist website, a postcard-writing campaign, and an all-night "read-in" with the slogan WE WILL NOT BE SHUSHED. Her efforts had doubtless helped restore some city aid, but there would still be cuts on top of the previous cuts, even as one closed branch, one less librarian, one shortened day of service would send more patrons streaming through her library's doors. Cutting services didn't make the need for them go away.

Now she was looking for work. Placement workshops and job recruitment had been offered by ALA at the conference, but it was "pretty sad," she said. Only fifteen recruiters were looking for librarians, and almost every librarian she knew was looking for a job. Some would end up overseas. Hong Kong was hiring, she'd heard. "See what the placement counselors give you?" she said, reaching under her name tag to flip down a white ribbon embossed in green letters with the words "Librarian for Hire." Then she tucked it back under her name. Why keep it hidden? Her boss was also at the conference, she explained, and it could be awkward if she ran into him while announcing her availability. She didn't want him to think she was giving up.

· · ·

David Ferriero, formerly head of the New York Public Library, now the tenth Archivist of the United States, sat in the stuffed chair in his elegant office in the National Archives, eight blocks from the convention center, and beamed. Behind his desk, a small-screen television let him monitor the Elena Kagan hearings—"a much bigger deal than mine," he said. He had been in office for six months and had leaned into his mission: to make the records of the government available to its people. Of course it was, by definition, a crazy job. Ferriero and his staff were supposed to capture, organize, preserve, and make accessible terabytes of digital records and the one billion pieces of paper the U.S. government generates every day. They had to figure out what was worth saving and then save it—including emails, BlackBerry messages, and government Facebook pages.

But this massive job wasn't enough, according to Ferriero. He believed that the civilians and scholars who engage with the archives could be valuable contributors to it, making discoveries and observations that were also worth preserving, such as the scholar who, while combing through centuries' old pension claims, found a unique proof of claim, a Revolutionary War diary. Ferriero wanted such observations saved, preserved, and organized as well.

"I want our agency to become a leader and innovator in all aspects of social media," he declared. Under his watch, the National Archives and Records Administration now hosts multiple blogs, Facebook pages, Twitter accounts, a Flickr page, a YouTube channel, and the "Open Government Idea Forum," which solicits citizens' suggestions about its efforts to support the open and transparent government decreed by President Obama. Ferriero has used his own blog, *AOTUS: Collector in Chief*, to promote the idea of citizen archivists.[1]

Hanging in frames outside his office were the personal documents his new staff unearthed from the archives: three letters written by David Ferriero as a boy to presidents Eisenhower, Kennedy, and Lyndon Johnson. He had no memory of writing those letters, but they are a source of pride: one citizen's voice reaching his government. Ferriero mentioned the millions of notes and emails that had been sent to Obama—an "overwhelming" number—then shifted from that daunting reality to enthusiasm for the future as he imagined an exhibit in which people could locate their own voices in the great clamor of history and find their own letters to the president preserved and displayed.

He left me in the beautiful Rotunda to squint at the Declaration of Independence under low lights, side by side with my fellow citizens. That night, catching up with my Twitter feed, I noticed that *Slate* was sponsoring a contest to boil the Declaration of Independence down to a 140-character tweet, including the hashtag "#tinydeclaration." (The eventual winner: "'Bye, George, we've got it.") I forwarded the announcement to Ferriero. His response: "Love it! Wish we had thought of it first!"

---

1 The recommended reading page for *AOTUS: Collector in Chief* includes this book, as well as *Infotopia*, *Wiki Government*, and *Abraham Lincoln: Vampire Hunter*.

Three years after the conference that introduced me to blogging librarians and book cart drills, I shouldered my way into a crowded conference room in the Washington, D.C., convention center. Most seats were taken, and librarians were already lining the sides, leaning against the wall or sitting on the floor with their backpacks and vendor bags. It was a smaller and more intense crowd than the one that had cheered for the book cart drills the night before.[2] This presentation, "Battledecks: the Rumble Royale," promised even more geek fun: librarians giving off-the-cuff presentations, using random and outrageous slides they'd never seen before—"Powerpoint meets Karaoke," or improv for infomaniacs.

The sport was new, with origins last year at the New Jersey state library conference, or perhaps the year before, at the techie conference, "South by Southwest," as an audience member shouted out. Six months earlier, at this year's ALA midwinter conference, a commons area set aside for unstructured meetings ("unconferences") had been the scene of a spontaneous showdown—fueled, rumor had it, by drunken librarians. By June 2010, it was organized enough to have a prominent place on the ALA calendar and an original logo, which incorporated an illustration of the first-prize tiara. Almost all of the contenders, most of the judges (including Jenny Levine and David Lee King), and many in the audience were blogging librarians, wired professionals who speak publicly about their calling on a regular basis. Here some would

2 The deserving winners of the book cart drill in 2010 were an inspired group of library science students from the University of Pittsburgh who dressed in skeleton costumes, spun book carts disguised as tombstones, and wafted and waltzed to Saint-Saëns' *Danse Macabre*.

face the ultimate test in spontaneous punditry: Could they speak coherently on the topic of change in libraries while absurd and funny visuals flashed behind them? Could they speak to the slides? Could they nail the jokes?

The nine contenders were introduced with fanfare—one wore a kilt, one made a grand entrance in the mask of a professional wrestler, one had just volunteered from the audience—then banished to a remote room. One by one they re-entered and took the stage. Lisa Carlucci Thomas, the "Iron Info Maiden" in four inch heels and flowing blond hair, demonstrated a breezy style as she addressed a slide of Arnold Schwarzenegger as Conan the Librarian. "Conan wants me to tell you that failure is an illusion. Remember that. If you're not sure, wear your leather belt to work." The slide of a little creature with a stunned look (a baby white owl?) was also no problem for Carlucci: "This is skeptical you," she said, to appreciative laughter. Bobbi ("Librarian by Day") Newman, who "has recently found the joy of going commando while presenting," had a slide in her deck that featured a pair of red high heels adorned with feathers. What do high heels have to do with change and the future of librarianship? "Everyone has a different comfort level," she said smoothly.

The visuals were the work of inspired librarians like Andy Woodworth and Jaime Corris Hammond, whose hand-drawn slide, "panflute flowchart," posed the question, "Do you need one?" A "yes" arrow pointed to a box that said "No, you don't." All answers led to the inevitable conclusion: "No panflute." When the laughter subsided, Jason Griffey looked at the image and mused, "This is very similar to the chart that says, 'Should you call a meeting?'"

But the slide that clinched victory and the first-place tiara for him showed an oversized geek in glasses and mustache with the headline *Do you have my stapler?* Griffey said confidently: "Everybody has one of these on staff, usually in the cataloging department." The uproar was immediate, laughter mixed with gasps. "No, you didn't!" someone shouted. "You know it's true," Griffey said.

I pulled on a bright red T-shirt emblazoned with the slogan VOTE FOR LIBRARIES and strolled up to the big rally on getaway day. People smiled benevolently, as if I were one of those good librarians who hosts story time and defends our right to read *Huckleberry Finn*. One woman said, "Great. Where do I vote?" and I was flummoxed, because public libraries are chartered in different ways: in some places citizens vote on their public library budgets, and in others they would have to petition government agencies or library boards. I shrugged and told her to write her representative. Later I asked a librarian for advice, and she started to explain the myriad structures and state variations on public library charters. There were municipal public libraries and public libraries that were also school district libraries . . . "You know," she finally said, "if people want to demonstrate their support, they should ask their librarians. Librarians know what kind of library they work at and how it's funded. They can tell them how to make their voices heard."

Of course. Ask your librarian. Always the right answer.

They gathered in the blazing sun that morning in view of the Capitol, more than a thousand librarians in red T-shirts, all fired up and waving signs that said, "The Cat in the Hat says, 'Branch Libraries Come Back!'" and "Libraries are the cornerstone of democracy." The public library is an increasingly threatened institution. In one year, the trickle of public libraries in financial straits has turned into a cascade: in cities like Boston, Dallas, New York, Las Vegas, Charlotte, Indianapolis, Los Angeles, and Newark; in the states of Illinois, Ohio, Florida, and New Jersey. California has cut so many positions for school librarians it's as if an entire profession dedicated to helping children compete in the wired world had been struck from the budget altogether. The money saved is modest at best; as the ALA points out, in the United States more money is spent on candy than on libraries.

Longtime library advocate Vernon Ehlers, a congressman from Michigan's third district, was one of the speakers. Asthmatic as a boy, he stayed home from school on many occasions and depended on his public library to help educate him and connect him to the world. He wasn't there to rile up the librarians with rhetoric, however. He was set to retire at the end of the year and felt compelled to give the librarians some parting advice: it wasn't enough that their cause was good and righteous. Their campaign wasn't about the justice of equal access to information, or the provisions that should be made for citizens who couldn't afford computers and Internet access; it had nothing to do with what was right and fair. "You have to get community support," the man said bluntly. "You have to get out there and campaign for local candidates who support libraries, and get them elected. You have to become politically astute and develop and support these candidates. Then the money will flow."

They had to become lobbyists, and then out-lobby those who want missile systems, bank bailouts, and subsidies for big sugar. Library advocates had to be canny and a good deal more ruthless if they wanted a bigger share of the pie for libraries. Ruthless? Don't make me laugh. Librarians are the last idealists. The proof surrounded me, these people waving signs, sweating in the summer sun, preparing to head up Capitol Hill to ask their senators and representatives to please vote for libraries, please require schools to have libraries and staff them, please fund the Library Services and Technology Act, please support a free and open Internet.

"Remember," the representative from the American Library Association reminded the sea of librarians as they prepared to meet with the politicians, "we aren't asking on our behalf. We are asking on behalf of those thousands behind us. We're asking on behalf of children, on behalf of the tens and hundreds of millions of people who use libraries to develop their skills and to find jobs...."

They aren't doing this for themselves, or each other. They're doing this for us.

ACKNOWLEDGMENTS

Among the many, many people who helped me research this book, a few helped me time and again, across months and years, well beyond any reasonable expectation: Jenna Freedman, Susan Hamburger, Wayne Hay, J. J. Jacobson, Kathryn Shaughnessy, and David Smith. They were patient with me—I knew nothing when I started—and they shared their knowledge, skills, and insights with grace and good cheer. I'm grateful to them beyond measure. They, like all my sources, did not know what I would end up writing, and it's my fault if anything has been garbled in the process.

I'm indebted to all the librarians mentioned in the book, many of whom did much more than their part in the narrative might suggest; I'm particularly grateful to Maurice (Mitch) Friedman and Siobhan Reardon. I would also like to thank the following people who were not mentioned but went to great lengths to help me: Elizabeth Bermel, Jane Marino, Sandra

Miranda, and Stephanie Sarnoff; the IT staff of WLS, especially Wilson Arana and Rob Caluori; the staffs of the Chappaqua, Mt. Pleasant, Ossining, and White Plains branches; the Westchester Library Association; and the WLS board, especially Dave Donelson.

Rebecca Guenther of the Library of Congress led me into the back rooms of cataloging and was a wonderful guide through Washington, D.C., and London.

Meredith Farkas and Rick Roche were especially helpful. Thanks to Robin K. Blum, Jill Cirasella, Meg Holle, David Lee King, Edward Morgan, Tom Peters, and LISNews. My correspondence with The Happy Villain was one of the pleasures of this project.

Thanks to those who helped me in Queens and Rome and weren't mentioned: Jean Davilus, Caroline Gozzer Fuchs, Cara McMahon, Dr. Anna Clemente Rosi, Blythe Roveland-Brenton, Joseph Sciortino, Angela Maria Bezerra Silva, Zeldi Trespeses, and Heather Wolcott. Thanks to the many who helped me navigate and interview in Second Life: Wrath Crosby, Mae Goldflake, Jack Granath, Trevor Hilder, Lorie Hyten, Jilly Kidd, Teofila Matova, Dennis Moser, Gareth Osler (Gareth Otsuko), Sonja Plummer-Morgan, and Sheila Webber, whom I met in London and who as Sheila Yoshikawa conducts a series of seminars on education and research in Second Life that helped me immeasurably. I could not have reconstructed the conversations and some of the events in this chapter without the technical assistance of my first friend in SL, Inigo Kamachi. I would not have survived my author appearances, or been able to navigate so many of the librarian encounters, without the kind help of Steven R. Harris, a/k/a Stolvano Barbosa.

Thanks to the staff of the New York Public Library who appear in this book, but also Paul Holdengräber, Kim Irwin, and Meg Semmler, who put on excellent programs, some of which I participated in; Isaac Gewirtz; and Herb Scher. Stewart Bodner was a great help. I could not have written this book without the benefit of the Frederick Lewis Allen Room.

I'm grateful also to Solveig De Sutter and the Society of American Archivists, and especially L. Rebecca Johnson Melvin, Michael Cogswell of the Louis Armstrong House and Museum, and Mary Ann Quinn. Nancy Adgent and her reading list were invaluable.

Mark Bartlett of the New York Society Library was a thoughtful and generous source. Kathy Jennings of Topeka and Shawnee County Public Library gave me a special tour, as did Joseph Shemtov of the Free Library of Philadelphia's Rare Books Department. Thanks to Larry Seims of PEN, David Sharp of BFI, Charles Warren, and the librarians of the Internet Public Library. Clifford Lynch of the Coalition for Networked Information generously shared his thoughts and insights. Rory McLeod gave me a whole day behind the scenes of the British Library, including its archives and its Coalition for Conservation; I'm so grateful to him and his colleagues, John Rhatigan and Alison Faraday. Thanks to Dottie Hiebing and Jason Kucsma of the excellent Metropolitan New York Library Council, the organizers of the Computers in Libraries conference, and the Center for Lesbian and Gay Studies and the City University of New York.

These lists do not include the scores and hundreds of archivists, librarians, clerks, pages, IT staff, and scholars who either helped me anonymously, prefer to remain anonymous, or have been inadvertently neglected here, to my great regret. Nor does it include scores of friends and family members who supported me, sent me clippings, and fed me, literally and figuratively, along the way, or any of the dear writers and editors who gave me advice, though Ben Cheever, Marcelle Clements, Lee Eisenberg, Esmeralda Santiago, and Larkin Warren improved chapters, and Susan Squire gave the complete manuscript her tireless and scrupulous attention.

I'm grateful to my agent, Chris Calhoun of Sterling Lord, and the good people of HarperCollins, especially my inspired editor, David Hirshey. Thanks as well to Jane Beirn, Milan Bozic, Shannon Ceci, Kayleigh George, Kate Hamill, George Quraishi, Virginia Stanley, and Nick Trautwein.

The generation behind me and the generation ahead, my children and my parents, are my motivators. Jackson, Carolyn, and Nick Fleder have, with grace and good humor, made space for this odd sibling. My parents, Dave and Dotty Johnson, taught me to love both books and librarians, and to follow my heart. That led me to this project, and it also led me to Rob Fleder, without whom this—all of it—would have been unthinkable.

NOTES

1. The Frontier

5 **I became interested in librarians while researching my first book:** The librarian and sailor with the phenomenal memory was Agnes Swift, who died in 2004, at the age of ninety-six. The map librarian was Walt Ristow, who died in 2006, at ninety-seven. The website marilynjohnson.net links to some extraordinary obituaries of librarians, including these.

12 **We know the first words uttered on the telephone:** The digital history I quoted here was Gregory S. Hunter's revised *Developing and Maintaining Practical Archives*.

2. Information Sickness

13 **If you don't know where to find a book:** WorldCat.org is brought to you by OCLC, which stands for Online Computer Library Center, Inc. It was founded by librarian Frederick G. Kilgour, who in 1967 had the bright idea to combine the catalog records of fifty-

four Ohio colleges (OCLC originally stood for Ohio College Library Center). OCLC is supposedly nonprofit, but some librarians lift their eyebrows at this. Not *every* library is in WorldCat. Libraries have to pay to join, and rather a lot, I'm told. Libraries pay to contribute their catalog records, then pay to use the records. Still, it's a very cool tool for those of us who need to find a book.

14 **Because I happened to be embedded in that big library:** Either I'm irrational about microfilm or librarians are. They all insist it is essential and remains stable for many years. I hate it with a passion. Elsewhere in this book I mention Nicholson Baker's *Double Fold*, the title of which refers to a library test to determine the brittleness of a paper item. A corner of a page was folded back and forth multiple times; if the paper didn't spring back, the book or newspaper would be deemed too fragile and deaccessioned. In the name of the double fold, untold books and, particularly, old print runs of newspapers were trashed, and microform versions substituted in their place. I appreciated *Double Fold*, and tried not to get too friendly with librarians who didn't appreciate it as well.

18 **I could have gone to Google:** I could have saved the web pages and then gone back and consulted them anytime—as long as my hardware and software remained current.

20 **Google couldn't answer the question:** Brian Herzog's blog, *Swiss Army Librarian*, is recommended for its bracing doses of reality and intriguing reference questions. Herzog is also, it seems, at least partially responsible for the handy calculator with which you can put a monetary value on the library services you use.

21 **Mosman Library, located near Sydney, Australia, sponsored a contest:** I am indebted to Kathryn Greenhill, who writes the blog *Librarians Matter*, for the tip to tune into the Mosman Library challenge.

3. On the Ground

This is a chapter about my own public libraries. I hadn't intended to stay in my own backyard, but I walked into the story, and consequently spent a great deal of time in the curious state of patron-reporter. I'm anything but objective. I walked into my first trustees meeting of the Westchester Library System, thinking I would be sitting in an audience, anonymously; I was not only the sole representative of the public in attendance, and knew, independently, four of the people there, but I was also the subject of one of the reports because I was slated to read at their annual authors luncheon.

There are thirty-eight libraries in WLS, but one, the White Plains Library, runs its own software.

32 **Carolyn Reznick and Maryanne Eaton had been on the job:** Carolyn Reznick later left Chappaqua to direct the Ruth Keeler Memorial Library in North Salem, also in the Westchester Library System.

38 **"Unfortunately, the move has been disastrous":** To be completely fair, the Insane Clown Posse songs are titled "If You Can't Beat 'Em Join 'Em" and "Dead Pumpkins" (along with "Toxic Love" and "Murda Cloak"). At any rate, the search algorithm has been fixed and the Insane Clown Posse no longer pops up ahead of the book.

45 **Hay and his staff, frustrated by all the money:** Working in one of the local libraries, I looked up to see a sign that listed all the things I couldn't do there. I was so freaked out I wrote them all down:
    NO Abusive language
    Animals
    Bare Feet
    Candy

Disturbing Noise

Feet on Furniture

Running

Sleeping

Smoking

Soliciting

Sports Equipment

Blogger Michael Stephens has a funny presentation mocking negative signs in libraries. I sympathize with the librarians who post signs saying *No Disturbing Noise* or *No Soliciting*. I can just imagine what compelled them to write these. But I wish I'd see lists telling me what I *can* do.

The Library Concept Center in Delft is called DOK for the three concepts it embraces: music (*Discotake*), the public library (*Openbare bibliotheek*), and art (*Kunst*).

4. The Blog People

51 **The ranting, mocking model prevailed:** *The Society for Librarians* Who Say "Motherfucker"* is a group blog, active since 2004, that has a number of rules, one of which states, "What happens at the SLWSM STAYS at the SLWSM." In other words, if library workers recognize coworkers by their rants, they should not rat them out. The asterisk in the title is explained: "Open to librarians; library associates, specialists, technicians, and paraprofessionals of all kinds; library school students; library aides and volunteers; and all of those who love libraries, or even just love a particular librarian. Welcome."

52 **People serious about the future of librarianship:** Graham Lavender is the librarian behind *The Inspired Library School Student.* "Five Weeks to a Social Library" is an excellent online course that could catch anyone up on social networking. It was devised by Meredith Farkas, Michelle Boule, Karen Coombs, Amanda

Etches-Johnson, Ellyssa Kroski, and Dorothea Salo, all blogging librarians. "23 Things" is another good online course, devised by Helene Blowers of the Public Library of Charlotte and Mecklenburg County in North Carolina to teach librarians the tools of Library 2.0 (Blowers has since moved to the Columbus Metropolitan Library in Ohio). Stephen Abrams's list, "43 Things I Might Want to Do This Year," challenges readers to teach themselves the tools of the Web by listing tasks they want to accomplish ("Get a Del.icio.us account and play with social bookmarking and tags").

57 **It also gave those of us with questions:** Jessamyn West's "Ubuntu @ the Library" is posted with its original soundtrack on Vimeo, which is how it should be viewed. She got a "scary letter about copyrighted music" from YouTube, so another soundtrack, not nearly as much fun, accompanies this video on that site.

5. Big Brother and the Holdout Company

67 **The PEN America gala was just like high school:** The Patriot Act is officially called The USA PATRIOT Act of 2001, which stands for Uniting and Strengthening America by Providing Appropriate Tools Required to Intercept and Obstruct Terrorism Act.

85 **During the height of the debate about the Patriot Act:** Jessamyn West published "Five *Technically* Legal Signs for Your Library (plus one)" on *librarian.net* in 2005. Here's another sample:

Organizations Who Have Not Stopped By This Week

1. Red Cross
2. Boy Scouts
3. United Way
4. ~~FBI~~
5. Rotary Club

7. To the Ramparts

116 **Zines represent a challenge:** Jim Danky was the mentor who advised Freedman about archival copies.

117 **She handed me a mini-zine:** Sarah Gentile conceived and created *Cite This Zine*.

118 **I curled up with a couple of librarian zines:** Library student Alycia Sellie created the Library Workers Zine Collection.

8. Follow That Tattooed Librarian

124 **The competition in 2007 was held in a hangar:** There are numerous postings on YouTube of librarian book-cart drills, all of which seem to have been recorded on cell phones. They look like cheesy, retro, amateur events. They're better in person.

126 **If *you* don't mention the stereotype, librarians will:** Nancy Pearl's program for the Washington Center for the Book, begun in 1998, has evolved into the One City One Book program, widespread in the United States. The Center for the Book at the Library of Congress tracks the books and communities that read them.

127 **From the description on Amazon of one of the many, many steamy books:** Jessamyn West has collected entertaining links to "The Famous Naked Librarians—Or Are They?" (are they librarians, that is; they're definitely naked).

127 **Tazmira and I had been Facebook friends:** The Facebook group Archivists Without Crippling Personality Disorders seems to have disbanded, alas.

129 **The phenomenon of smart, funny, cool librarians:** Gary Shapiro wrote "For New-Look Librarians, Head to Brooklyn," in the *New York Sun*, July 5, 2007. The *Times*'s story, "A Hipper Crowd of Shushers," appeared three days later.

9. Wizards of Odd

137 **I first learned about this world:** Erica Firment of *Librarian Avengers* was formerly known as Erica Olsen.

143 **Hypatia's profile noted that she was lesbian and partnered:** The librarian behind Hypatia Dejavu left the job where her boss despised Second Life. She is now a reference librarian at a branch of the New York Public Library.

145 **Hypatia was waiting in the library plaza:** In 2008, the librarians of Second Life launched their own publication, *RezLibris*, archived at rezlibris.com.

152 **Each success made them bolder:** After three years and eight months organizing and seeding library projects in Second Life, and following a 17 percent cut in their home consortium's budget, Alliance Virtual Library passed the management of Info Island and its library initiative to a group of three volunteer librarian-avatars, Hypatia Dejavu, Abbey Zenith, and Rocky Vallejo (Bill Sowers of the State Library of Kansas) at the end of 2009. The new administrators will be know as the Community Virtual Library. Lori Bell will continue as their adviser.

158 **In the blunter, more prosaic, other world:** J. J. Jacobson is now Associate Curator for American Culinary History at the William L. Clements Library at the University of Michigan.

10. Gotham City

I was entwined and entangled with the New York Public Library, even while reporting on it for this book. I applied for but didn't receive a Cullman Center Fellowship, but I was given a key to the Frederick Lewis Allen Room, where I spent many happy hours writing and reading the books and articles that David Smith and the other librarians had gathered for me. I helped Paul Holdengräber put on two programs in the Trustees Room of the library while in the midst of writing this book, one a tribute to the fiction editor Rust Hills, the other, a panel on the art of the obituary with Ann Wroe, the writer of *The Economist*'s obituaries.

173 **But Smith was an indefatigable reference librarian:** The "black book catalog" is the 800-volume *Dictionary Catalog of the Research Libraries of the New York Public Library*, which contains photographic reproductions of the cards in the 6,000+ catalog drawers in the Public Catalog Room.

184 **It was a beautiful moment:** In an extraordinary gesture from David Ferriero and Paul LeClerc, David Smith was honored as a Library Lion the November after his retirement; former honorees include Philip Roth, Elie Wiesel, Salman Rushdie, and Oprah Winfrey. He has not given up the idea of an Office of Writers' Services.

192 **And the library is run like a philanthropy:** Zahra M. Baird, now the teen librarian at the Chappaqua Public Library in New York, left her job running a branch in the South Bronx in 2000, for which she was paid $31,000 a year; "I didn't choose this career to become rich," she told the *New York Times*, "but I didn't take a vow of poverty, either." Starting salary in 2009 for a senior librarian was $42,000.

193 **The website refers to the tangle of civic and philanthropic funds:** See the website Driven by Boredom for the story "The Donnell Library Center: A Eulogy in Pictures."

196 **But, like library administrators everywhere:** In 2009, David Ferriero was nominated by Barack Obama as Archivist of the United States.

11. What's Worth Saving?

215 **Her archives are gold.:** Toni Morrison personally told me she had been so determined to complete a thought once that, even after the child in her arms (her son Slade) threw up on her writing paper, she continued writing the sentence. I could relate. She had returned my call for an interview about Oprah's book club for *Life* magazine. I was frying hamburgers for my children at the time, and scrawled the notes from the interview through spatters of grease.

239 **I tacked questions at the back of every interview:** "We're talking about terabytes . . ." came from a wonderfully obscene screed by Jason Scott on his blog, *ASCII*.

242 **After the team gathered all these items:** Liz Madden points out that the September 11 Digital Archive does indeed live on, but is currently being served from its original location: http://911digitalarchive.org.

12. The Best Day

250 **I'd see the library in my own time:** I returned to the Darien Library a couple months after it opened, in March 2009, when it hosted an "unconference" on the future of the library. Some of the busiest librarians on the Internet were in attendance, including Kathryn Greenhill, then the emerging-technologies specialist at Murdoch University Library in Australia. John Blyberg introduced her by saying she "has never been to the States but she already knows everyone." That was not much of an exaggeration; most of us in the room read her blog and followed her on Twitter. The presentations and free-form discussions of the day were live-streamed, so librarians from near and far could attend by videoconference. There were about fifty people there, and many of them were blogging the event as it happened. And when Greenhill wasn't onstage, she was thumb-

ing her smart phone, summing up the discussion for her Twitter network.

Long after I and all those smart library students and librarians had left, Greenhill, Blyberg, and blogger Cindi Trainor used their notes from the day to draft a vision of their profession for the future. They called it "The Darien Statements on the Library and Librarians," and it was grand: "The purpose of the Library is to preserve the integrity of civilization," it began. "Why we do things will not change, but how we do them will. . . . If the Library is to fulfill its purpose in the future, librarians must commit to a culture of continuous operational change, accept risk and uncertainty as key properties of the profession, and uphold service to the user as our most valuable directive."

The list of things librarians must do to remain relevant included: "Promote openness, kindness, and transparency among libraries and users. . . . Choose wisely what to stop doing. . . . Adopt technology that keeps data open and free, abandon technology that does not. . . . Trust each other and trust the users." Naturally, it excited the interest of librarians around the blogosphere and drew the mockery of the Annoyed Librarian. "I Heart Librarian Manifestos," she wrote.

I like the idea behind the "culture of continuous operational change"—the embrace of the shifting world—and I also like the statement that service is the key part of the public librarians' job. It's a crazy, messy moment in the information era, but these librarians are lighting a path through it, and what better standard could they employ than *usefulness*?

SELECT BIBLIOGRAPHY

Abram, Stephen, Judith A. Siess, and Jonathan Lorig. *Out Front with Stephen Abram*. Chicago: American Library Association, 2007.

Abramson, Larry, and Maria Godoy. "The Patriot Act: Key Controversies." NPR. February 14, 2006.

Ambacher, Bruce I. *Thirty Years of Electronic Records*. Lanham, Maryland: Scarecrow Press, 2003.

Arnot, Chris. "Stemming Flow of Literary Heritage Across the Pond." *The Guardian*. July 15, 2008.

Baker, Nicholson. *Double Fold: Libraries and the Assault Against Paper*. New York: Vintage, 2002.

Basbanes, Nicholas A. *Patience and Fortitude: A Roving Chronicle of Book People, Book Places, and Book Culture*. New York: HarperCollins, 2001.

———. *Every Book Its Reader: The Power of the Printed Word to Stir the World*. New York: HarperCollins, 2005.

Bell, Lori, and Rhonda B. Trueman. *Virtual Worlds, Real Libraries: Librarians and Educators in Second Life and Other Multi-user Virtual Environments*. Medford, New Jersey: Information Today, 2008.

Benton Foundation. *Buildings, Books, and Bytes: Libraries and Communities in the Digital Age*. Washington, D.C.: Benton Foundation, 1998.

Boekesteijn, Erik. "Discover Innovations at DOK, Holland's 'Library Concept Center.'" *Marketing Library Services*. March/April 2008.

Boellstorff, Tom. *Coming of Age in Second Life: An Anthropologist Explores the Virtually Human*. Princeton: Princeton University Press, 2008.

Boutin, Paul. "The Archivist: Brewster Kahle Made a Copy of the Internet. Now He Wants Your Files." *Slate*. April 7, 2005.

Brewerton, Antony. "Wear Lipstick, Have a Tattoo, Belly-dance, Then Get Naked: The Making of a Virtual Librarian." *Impact: Journal of the Career Development Group*. November/December 1999.

Carlson, Scott. "Young Librarians, Talkin' 'Bout Their Generation." *Chronicle of Higher Education*. October 19, 2007.

Cirasella, Jill, and Mariana Regalado, guest eds. "LPP Special Issue: Libraries and Google." *Library Philosophy and Practice*. June 2007.

Cohen, Daniel, and Roy Rosenzweig. *Digital History: A Guide to Gathering, Preserving, and Presenting the Past on the Web*. Philadelphia: University of Pennsylvania Press, 2005.

Cowan, Alison Leigh. "At Stake in Court: Using the Patriot Act to Get Library Records." *The New York Times*. September 1, 2005; "Hartford Libraries Watch as U.S. Makes Demands," September 2, 2005; "Connecticut Librarians See Lack of Oversight as Biggest Danger in Antiterror Law," September 3, 2005; "Plaintiffs Win Round in Patriot Act Lawsuit," September 10, 2005; "Librarians Must Stay Silent in

Patriot Act Suit, Court Says," September 21, 2005; "Judges Question Patriot Act in Library and Internet Case," November 3, 2005; "A Court Fight to Keep a Secret That's Long Been Revealed," November 18, 2005; "Books for Lending, Data for Taking," November 20, 2005; "Librarian Is Still John Doe, Despite Patriot Act Revision," March 21, 2006; "Four Librarians Finally Break Silence in Records Case," May 31, 2006; "U.S. Ends a Yearlong Effort to Obtain Library Records Amid Secrecy in Connecticut," June 27, 2006.

Craig, David J. "Overbooked?" *Columbia Magazine*. Spring 2008.

Crawford, Walt. *The Liblog Landscape, 2007–2008: A Lateral Look.* Mountain View, California: Cites & Insights Book, 2009.

Dain, Phyllis. *The New York Public Library: A History of Its Founding and Early Years.* New York: New York Public Library, 1972.

Darnton, Robert. "The Library in the New Age." *New York Review of Books.* June 12, 2008.

Dodge, Chris. "The New Monastic Librarians." *Utne Reader.* July/August 2005.

Eberhart, George M. *The Whole Library Handbook 4: Current Data, Professional Advice, and Curiosa about Libraries and Library Services.* Chicago: American Library Association, 2006.

Estabrook, Leigh S., et al. "The Benton Report: A Response." *Library Trends.* Summer 1997.

Farkas, Meredith G. *Social Software in Libraries: Building Collaboration, Communication, and Community Online.* Medford, New Jersey: Information Today, 2007.

Foster, Andrea L. "Strains and Joys Color Mergers Between Libraries and Tech Units." *Chronicle of Higher Education.* January 18, 2008.

Freedman, Jenna. "Veteran Librarians." *Library Journal.* July 2–23, 2009 (in four parts).

———. *Lower East Side Librarian Winter Solstice Shout Out* [zine]. Issues No. 2–8. New York: 2002–2008.

Goodman, Amy, and David Goodman. *Standing Up to the Madness: Ordinary Heroes in Extraordinary Times.* New York: Hyperion, 2008.

Gordon, Jane. "In Patriots' Cradle, the Patriot Act Faces Scrutiny." *The New York Times.* April 24, 2005.

Greenhouse, Steven. "Forlorn and Forgotten in the Stacks; Low Pay Is Driving Many Librarians Out of New York City." *The New York Times.* March 14, 2000.

Hsu, Hua. "File Under Other: How Do Libraries—Institutions That By Nature Require a Strict, Stately Style of Micromanagement—Assimilate These Self-published and Occasionally Category-defying Dispatches from the Cultural Hinterlands?" *The Boston Globe.* May 6, 2007.

Hunnicutt, Susan C. "Defining Cybrarian." *MLA Forum.* 2(2) May 7, 2003.

Hunter, Gregory S. *Developing and Maintaining Practical Archives: A How-To-Do-It Manual.* New York: Neal-Schuman Publishers, 2003.

Josey, E. J., and Ann Allen Shockley. *Handbook of Black Librarianship.* Littleton, Colorado: Libraries Unlimited, Inc., 1977.

Kaplan, Hank. "Too Much Ring 'Rage' in De Niro's LaMotta." *The Sweet Science.* September 30, 2005.

Kelly, Stuart. *The Book of Lost Books: An Incomplete History of All the Great Books You Will Never Read.* New York: Random House, 2005.

Levy, David M. *Scrolling Forward: Making Sense of Documents in the Digital Age.* New York: Arcade Publishing, 2001.

Lichtblau, Eric. "F.B.I., Using Patriot Act, Demands Library's Records." *The New York Times.* August 26, 2005.

Lohr, Steve. "Libraries Wired, and Reborn." *The New York Times.* April 22, 2004.

Lubetzky, Seymour. *Cataloging Rules and Principles: A Critique of the A.L.A. Rules for Entry and a Proposed Design for Their Revision.* Washington, D.C.: Library of Congress, Processing Department, 1953.

Madden, Liz. "Digital Curation at the Library of Congress: Lessons Learned from American Memory and the Archive Ingest and Handling Test." *International Journal of Digital Curation.* 3(2) 2008.

Max, D. T. "Final Destination: Why Do the Archives of So Many Great Writers End Up in Texas?" *The New Yorker.* June 11, 2007.

Mooney, Ted. *Easy Travel to Other Planets.* New York: Farrar, Straus and Giroux, 1981.

Murray, Janet Horowitz. *Hamlet on the Holodeck: The Future of Narrative in Cyberspace.* New York: Free Press, 1997.

Oder, Norman. "ALA, Allied Organizations Ask Congress to Revise Patriot Act." *Library Journal.* April 9, 2009.

Pearl, Nancy. *Book Lust.* Seattle: Sasquatch Books, 2003.

Peters, Tom. "Barnacles on the Ship of Librarianship." *ALA TechSource.* December 15, 2008.

Pogrebin, Robin. "Blackstone Chief Executive Pledges $100 Million to New York Public Library," originally published as "For $100 Million, a Library Card and Perhaps His Name in Stone." *The New York Times.* March 11, 2008; "British Architect to Redesign City Library," October 22, 2008.

Roberts, Sam. "The Library's Helpful Sage of the Stacks." *The New York Times.* December 31, 2007.

San Diego, Jenny. *Not Sorry* [zine]. Issue No. 3. Portland: 2005.

Santora, Marc. "After Big Gift, a New Name for the Library." *The New York Times.* April 23, 2008.

Sara and Jenn. *Riot Librarrrian* [zine]. Issue No. 1. Chicago: 2002.

Shapiro, Susin. "Creeps and Assholes: Character Is Destiny." *The Village Voice.* Issue 24. New York: June 4, 1979.

Shirky, Clay. *Here Comes Everybody: The Power of Organizing Without Organization.* New York: Penguin Press, 2008.

Slotnik, Daniel E. "Public Library's Online Catalog Causes Delays in Troubled Debut." *The New York Times.* July 7, 2009.

Steinhauer, Jennifer. "A Literary Legend Fights for a Local Library." *The New York Times.* June 19, 2009.

Weinberger, David. *Everything Is Miscellaneous: The Power of the New Digital Disorder.* New York: Times Books, 2007.

West, Celeste, and Elizabeth Katz, eds. *Revolting Librarians.* San Francisco: Bootlegger Press, 1972.

West, Jessamyn, and K. R. Roberto, eds. *Revolting Librarians Redux: Radical Librarians Speak Out.* Jefferson, North Carolina: McFarland & Co., 2003.

Willing, Richard. "With Only a Letter, FBI Can Gather Private Data." *USA Today.* July 6, 2006.

Woodsworth, Anne. *Library Cooperation and Networks: A Basic Reader.* New York: Neal-Schuman Publishers, 1991.

Books by MARILYN JOHNSON

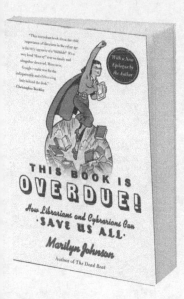

THIS BOOK IS OVERDUE!
How Librarians and Cybrarians Can Save Us All
ISBN 978-0-06-143161-6 (paperback)

Tracing the history of librarians from Dewey to digital, Johnson explores the next wave of the industry—what the cybrarians call Library 2.0—and how this new paradigm of archiving will affect the preservation of our culture.

"Topical, witty. . . . Johnson's wry report is a must-read for anyone who's used a library in the past quarter century."
—*Publishers Weekly* (starred review)

THE DEAD BEAT
Lost Souls, Lucky Stiffs, and the Perverse Pleasures of Obituaries
ISBN 978-0-06-075876-9 (paperback)

A light-hearted and hilarious look at the history and practice of "the ultimate human-interest story," *The Dead Beat* surveys the cult and culture behind the obituary page, and chronicles the unusual lives we don't quite appreciate until they're gone.

"[A] fascinating book about the art, history, and subculture of obituary writing. . . . Johnson's analysis of the form . . . [and] her accounts of the culture of obituary lovers is downright amazing."
—*New York Times Book Review*

DEC 2021

CPSIA information can be obtained
at www.ICGtesting.com
Printed in the USA
LVHW041730171121
703614LV00015B/2076